ONE OF THE BOYS

ONE OF THE BOYS

HOW TO SUCCEED AS A WOMAN IN A MALE-DOMINATED FIELD

KATIE ROGERS

NEW DEGREE PRESS

ONE OF THE BOYS

How to Succeed as a Woman in a Male-Dominated Field

ISBN   978-1-64137-155-1   *Paperback*

         978-1-64137-156-8   *Ebook*

To all of the women dominating in male-dominated fields.

CONTENTS

INTRODUCTION

———

"I want little girls to grow up knowing they can do anything, even play football."

—JEN WELTER, ARIZONA CARDINALS COACH

* * *

What comes to mind when you think of landing on the moon? Likely you think of Neil Armstrong and Buzz Aldrin, and their "one small step for man." Maybe you think of the American flag that they placed there. It is unlikely, however, that you think of Margaret Hamilton. In fact, you probably have never heard of her. Yet without her, that first moon landing would not have happened.

Margaret Hamilton was the woman behind the scenes that enabled Armstrong and Aldrin to reach the moon. She was the engineer who developed the necessary software for Apollo 11 to successfully land. She earned NASA's Exceptional Space Act award. She literally invented the term "software engineering."[1] Yet most people have never even heard of her.

When asked about the relationship between the men and the women working in computer programming at the time, Margaret Hamilton expressed that men were always the majority in the room. She explained how even though during the Apollo mission and on her other projects she was mostly surrounded by men, the mission of the project really transcended gender and everyone "worked side by side to solve the challenging problems and to meet the critical deadlines."[2] Like many women you will hear from in this book, Margaret was so focused on her work, that it never really occurred to her how outnumbered by men she was. She noted that they were far more likely to notice someone's specialty than their gender.

"We concentrated on our work much more than whether one was male or female. We were more likely to notice if someone

1   Creighton, Jolene. 2018. "Margaret Hamilton: The Untold Story Of The Woman Who Took Us To The Moon". *Futurism.* https://futurism.com/margaret-hamilton-the-untold-story-of-the-woman-who-took-us-to-the-moon.

2   Ibid.

was a first floor or second floor person, a hardware or software guy, or what area someone was specializing in, e.g., man-machine interface, operating system, error detection and recovery, or in an application specific area."[3]

* * *

Plenty of women have achieved greatness in their lives. But one of the unique aspects of female achievement is the accomplishments that a woman earns when she does so in an industry, arena, sport, or activity that is dominated primarily or exclusively by men.

When a woman is in a male-dominated field, it is easy for her to feel all alone or left behind. Sometimes this is because the men don't want her there at all, but it is generally because men are not always thinking about how their actions are impacting the women that they work with and don't consider the struggles that women have to go through.

Even though more and more women are entering traditionally male-dominated fields, there is still a severe lack of female leadership across the board. There are only 24 female CEOs of Fortune 500 companies. That is less than 5%. That

---

3   Ibid.

means that the leadership of the top 500 companies is 95% male.[4]

A recent *New York Times* article came out about all of the different job roles that had more men by the same name than women in total in the role. There are more CEOs of Fortune 500 companies named James than there are women CEOs. There are more senators named John than there are Republican female senators. There are more Democratic governors named John than there are women governors. There are more male top movie directors named Michael and James than there are women directors.[5] The list goes on.

This illustrates a massive problem in the workforce. A lack of women in leadership leads to a lack of diversity at the upper levels of companies. This lack of diversity makes it exceptionally difficult for companies to create cultures that are welcoming to a diverse set of employees. As illustrated in my stories of being left behind by men, it is challenging for people to consider problems and situations that they do not experience themselves. That is why more women and other minorities need to assume leadership roles in order to make the workplace more equitable for everyone.

---

4   Miller, Claire, Kevin Quealy, and Margot Sanger-Katz. 2018. "The Top Jobs Where Women Are Outnumbered By Men Named John". *The New York Times* https://www.nytimes.com/interactive/2018/04/24/upshot/women-and-men-named-john.html.

5   Ibid.

When men are in charge of everything, it creates a hyper-masculine culture that can make it exceedingly difficult for women to break into. It also forces women to constantly need to communicate in the way that men do in order to be heard and respected.

* * *

Has any woman reading this book ever been out somewhere with a group of men—as the only woman in the group?

If you have, you probably know that unless you are married to or dating one of them (or one of them is hoping to date you), they will leave you alone without a second thought.

In fact, even if you are dating or married, there is *still* a really good chance they›ll leave you.

I have been left by myself at parties, sporting events, and other places when I chose to go out with a group of male friends.

It is easy for me to get angry in these situations. I always look out for my friends and I expect that they do the same for me. This has never been a problem with my female friends, but definitely is when it comes to male friends.

At first blush, you could say "what jerks." But I am convinced that most of the time; this is a product of ignorance rather than intention. I believe this tends to happen because men don't realize what they are doing. They often do not take into consideration how a woman is feeling. If a guy gets left behind, it is no big deal for them, but for a woman it can be a very big deal.

I recently attended a sporting event with some male friends. We were standing on the sidelines, all watching a sports team of which they themselves are a part (they just happened to not be playing in that particular game). At the end of the game, they all hopped over the barrier and onto the field, leaving me standing there all alone. This was not them trying to be mean, rather they were just totally oblivious to the fact that they had left me in the dust.

Now this particular situation did not leave me in any danger, but nevertheless it still was not a good feeling to be abandoned like that. In some cases, however, this lack of awareness is extremely dangerous.

There was an occasion where I attended a party with a group of all male friends. While at the party, a boy that I was acquainted with (but definitely was not friends with) began harassing me. I tried to handle the situation on my own, but he would not leave me alone. His behavior made me extremely uncomfortable and because I had many mutual friends with this boy, I was worried about causing too much of a scene (this in itself is an entirely different issue for women— the fact that I was more worried about what people would think of me for speaking up against this boy for his behavior rather than how they might react to the boy's actual behavior is extremely concerning). Anyway, because I couldn't resolve the situation on my own, I found one of my male friends and asked him for help. I explained what was going on and why I was uncomfortable. Instead of sticking with me for the night or removing me from the situation like a female friend probably would have, the guy friend I asked for help told me that it was fine and I had nothing to worry about, entirely ignoring my discomfort with the situation. Again, this was not him being cruel, rather it was just his inability to comprehend how I was feeling, as he had never experienced something like that before.

When going anywhere, women typically look out for one another. They will wait as long as necessary to ensure no one gets left behind. If a woman sees someone looking uncomfortable, they will often try to intervene in some way. This empathy for others comes from understanding the types of issues that women face. Men do not face many of the same issues as women, and therefore do not consider how others are feeling or the ramifications of their actions.

These stories aren't meant to make you angry at men and blame them for all of society's problems, rather I am describing examples that illustrate how men tend not to understand women's experiences, thoughts, and feelings. This is an incredibly important point when discussing women in male-dominated fields.

* * *

How can women thrive in fields dominated by men?

I asked that question of more than 100 women, and no one was able to offer me much more than anecdotes and general advice. There is no framework, no book, and no playbook for the game.

So I've decided to write one.

This book is designed to offer a framework based on research and interviews with dozens of women who have survived and thrived in a male-dominated world, industry or sport. In this book you'll hear the incredible stories and approaches of women including:

- How an executive in the tech industry overcame a male coworker who brought her to a strip club as a power play
- How a construction project manager learned to fit in with her male coworkers

- How female weightlifters earned the respect of the men at their gyms
- How a woman tackled playing for a collegiate men's football team
- How a college professor dealt with issues of unfair promotions and pay
- How an engineer from MIT has managed to be one of the few women in her entire industry

And what I've found is that the approach for these women relies on four core elements:

- Mindset
- Actions
- Words
- Community

Whether you're taking a job in a male-dominated field, playing in a co-ed sport, getting involved in the dating world (which yes also happens to be a male-dominated activity), or attempting to break a barrier, these four elements are the core to succeeding in your own journey to 'play with the boys.'

* * *

As someone with more male friends than female friends, I have constantly dealt with interacting with men. It honestly can be considered an art form more than a science sometimes.

It all started for me as a little kid. Growing up, I began training in martial arts around the age of five. This led me to become a pretty tough kid and to constantly be surrounded by a lot of boys. As I got older, a lot of my closest friends were boys, which was fairly abnormal for a girl. Most kids go through a phase where they think the other gender is icky. Not me.

I had no problem spending time with boys, playing rough, and laughing and teasing along with all of them. I always fit in well with the boys, but as I grew up I definitely noticed some challenges that come with being constantly surrounded by boys and men.

There were countless occasions where guy friends of mine would assume that I couldn't do something as well as they could because I was a girl. Whether it be throwing a ball, doing a karate move, or doing a physics problem in school, I have heard "Are you sure you can do that?", "Do you want some help?", and "I'm going to be way better at this than you" more times than I care to remember. Even worse, I have had many experiences where boys have just assumed that I won't want to do something because of my gender.

In college, a lot of my male friends play pick-up basketball games in our school's gym. Typically, they do not even consider inviting me to play; however, one day I finally scored an invite when I happened to be hanging out with one of them when they decided to go play. When we got to the gym, the two largest guys were the team captains. They began picking teams. I was not at all surprised they picked me last. I have been underestimated in physical tasks by boys throughout my entire life, so it was unsurprising they didn't expect much from me on the court. After we played the first game, we decided to switch teams. I was the first player picked.

In martial arts, I was constantly challenged by the boys in class, particularly when it came to any portions of training where we would hit each other. Initially, many of the boys treated me differently. They wouldn't hit me as hard as they would hit the other boys in the class and they assumed that I could not hit as hard as they could.

I quickly proved them wrong.

I was able to hang with them in everything that we did and was often the top performer. I learned to hit and spar kids much larger than I was in a very effective manner.

I may or may not have even caused a boy or two to cry.

I never cried once.

* * *

Something I have learned along the way is that as a woman dealing with men, you have to be extremely assertive and unafraid to verbally spar with them a bit. In order to communicate successfully with boys, you need to speak in the same ways that they do. They don't take any shit from each other and neither should you! When boys say something out of line or challenge your ability to do something, you need to readily stand up for yourself. It sucks that you have to prove yourself to them, but that is how you gain their respect.

I want this book to help other girls who have found themselves surrounded by boys and men to navigate the sometimes complex landscape that being the only woman can create. It highlights the experiences of a variety of women from a number of different fields where they are surrounded by men. I hope that this book can inspire women who may be a little intimidated to keep pushing through so they can make it to the tops of their industries and make the workplace better for the women who follow them.

HOW TO READ
THIS BOOK

—

This book is meant to be helpful for **YOU**. Everyone is different and will use this book in a different way. Maybe you are looking to take your time and read it cover to cover, in order, to really hear the different stories and fully understand the full landscape. You may, on the other hand, be looking for a specific topic or section of the book and just be reading that part. Likely, you fall somewhere in between. This section is intended to gauge how this book can best serve you and provide a playbook personalized for you so that you can get the most out of the time you spend combing the pages.

This book is broken up into four parts— Mindset, Actions, Words, and Community. Each of these sections contains different stories meant to give you a glimpse into how women have been challenged in these areas and how they have overcome these challenges. Take the assessment below to discover the best way to utilize these sections to help you achieve your own goals.

ASSESSMENT

ONE OF THE BOYS reader assessment

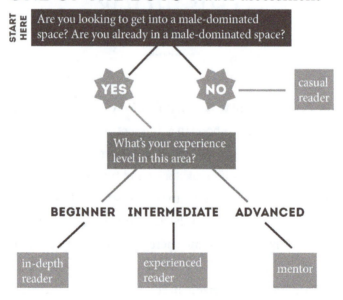

START HERE Are you looking to get into a male-dominated space? Are you already in a male-dominated space?

YES **NO** — casual reader

What's your experience level in this area?

BEGINNER **INTERMEDIATE** **ADVANCED**

in-depth reader   experienced reader   mentor

RESULTS

After taking the assessment to determine the best way for you to read this book, check out your personalized playbook below.

CASUAL READER

If you got casual reader, you likely are reading this book purely out of interest and to learn something. You may be considering entering into some sort of male-dominated space, but don't have any specific goals or plans yet. You also may be a man reading this to gain the perspective of what it is like for women who enter into male-dominated areas.

If this is the case, your best bet is to take your time and read this book in order, at your leisure. Take in all of the different stories and experiences that the women I interviewed have had and as you read, try to consider how similar experiences may be applicable in your own lives. Try to find at least one or two stories that speak to you in some way. Think about experiences you may have had or experiences that a family member or friend may have had and how those experiences were impactful.

As you reflect on these stories, challenge some of the stereotypes that have been engrained in your brain throughout your life. Next time a girl takes charge of a team you are working on, applaud her leadership abilities, rather than silently complaining to yourself about how bossy she is. When you see a man interrupting a woman who is speaking or ignoring what she is saying, challenge yourself to speak up. We need more people in the world who are constantly aware and thinking about how others are experiencing the same events we are, but in different ways. Be sure to check out Chapter 9, which discusses this issue in the context of diversity.

The bottom line is the best thing you can take from this book is how to be more aware of the different ways in which people experience the same events. After reading this, I hope you will be more in tune with how others can be affected by actions you may have never even noticed before.

IN-DEPTH READER

It sounds like you are about to enter the journey of entering a male-dominated field. Boy is this the book for you. The best way for you to take all there is to offer from this book is to read the whole damn thing. Yes, I mean cover to cover. And I do not mean that you should skim it. I mean really, actively read it. As you read each of the sections, challenge yourself to apply the stories and advice to your own life and your own situation. Determine how each chapter is applicable to your personal situation and how you can use the stories from the women in each of the chapters to create a better experience for yourself as you enter your chosen field. I would even recommend grabbing a notebook to jot down your thoughts as you read. This will help you keep track of what you are thinking and what you learn. It can be helpful to come back to when you are having a rough time or if you come across an obstacle down the road.

Start by reading the Mindset section. This section is a great primer for someone looking to get into a male-dominated field. It will help to set your expectations and get your head in the right space for the challenges ahead. While reading this section, reflect on how your current thoughts compare to the expectations set up in these chapters. Do you already have a similar mindset toward what is presented by the stories in this section? If not, figure out where the differences lie? Use this to determine how you will close the gap so that you are mentally prepared for your expedition. Be sure to note anything that surprises you, along with anything you see as being relevant to your own journey.

After you have worked through the Mindset chapters, work your way to the Action section. This part of the book will teach you how to be strong and show people what you are made of. These stories feature women facing major obstacles, many of which you are likely to face yourself, and talk about ways that did (and didn't) work to overcome them. When reading this section focus heavily on the titles of the chapters, as they offer some key points to remember as you come to tough spots on your journey. First, "Be Confident." You will not be successful if you do not believe in yourself. As you read Chapter 4, consider the things that you are really good at. What are your strong suits? How can you apply these strengths to make you successful in your endeavor? Then, "Stand Up for Yourself." In Chapter 5, think back to times that you may not of stood up for something that you probably should have. It can be something to do with gender, or it can just be a situation in which you should have stood up for yourself or someone else but didn't. Why didn't you act in this situation? What would you do differently if something like that were to happen again? Try to visualize what sticking up for yourself might look like so that it is easier for you to do it in real life when the time comes. Finally, "Take Risks and Persist." Use this chapter to reflect on risks you may have taken in the past. Would you deem them successful or not? If it was a success, what made you able to be successful? If not, what could you have done differently? Now apply this to the future. Consider what possible risks you may need to take in order to reach your goals and how to tackle those risks before you can get there. Really use the stories in these chapters to inspire yourself to really go for your goals.

As you enter the Words section, think about the importance of the words and language that you use. This section will not only help you communicate in male-dominated environments, but will also teach you to "Break the Locker Room" that is oh-so-common in groups of males, particularly in areas that have been dominated by men for a long time.

Finally, as you finish the book with the Community section, use the book to determine how you will create a community for yourself in your industry. No one is going to do it for you, so this is very much something you will need to do on your own. As you read, consider if there is anyone you feel could be a good mentor for you. Whom can you go to for help, guidance, and advice as you progress towards your goals? Keep your mind open. It could be another woman you look up to, but it doesn't have to be. Plenty of successful women have had impactful male mentors. Choose a person (or people) you admire and really connect with. Reflect on how you can build a relationship with people that fit your vision of a good mentor.

Once you finish reading, go out and do it! Take everything that you have learned and thought about throughout your experience reading this book and put it to work. And do not forget to come back to this book (and the notes that you hopefully took) when you need a little inspiration.

EXPERIENCED READER

If you got experienced reader, you most likely have entered some male-dominated space, but may need a little boost to get where you are trying to go. Obviously feel free to read the whole book or any parts that you find interesting or that may be specifically applicable to you. Your playbook, though, is to really focus on the Words and Community sections. Given that you are already involved in a male-dominated space, you likely already have had many experiences that have built up your mindset and confidence. The Words portion can help you to refine the way that you communicate with the men in your network and can provide you with tools to further build your relationships and insert yourself into the group. The Community section will provide you with ways to start forging your own community. It will also help you begin helping other women join the area that you dominated. As you read these sections reflect on the obstacles you may have encountered so far. What challenges have you faced? How have you worked to overcome them? What could you have done differently that may have worked better? What would you have liked to know before you entered the space?

You can use the answers to these questions to better yourself moving forward, as well as to help other women succeed in your field.

MENTOR

If you got mentor, you are likely the perfect candidate to be helping the next generation of women looking to enter your field. You can read whatever parts of the book look interesting to you, as there are little tidbits about mentorship throughout, but really focus on Part 4, the Community section. This section highlights the importance of mentors and will offer you suggestions as to how to help future generations of young women to be able to achieve success in your field.

Really use the Community portion to reflect on the people who helped you become successful and use this reflection to determine the best ways you can go about mentoring others. What mentors have you had? Who has been most influential in your life in terms of your field? Why was this person so influential? What elements of their mentorship could you channel in your quest to mentor others? Did you have any mentors that used tactics that you did not like or found were not helpful? If so, how can you be sure to avoid making these same mistakes with those that you mentor?

Thinking about these questions as you read will help you figure out the best way that you can serve the next generation of young women thinking about entering your field of expertise.

Also be sure to take a look at Chapter 9, which explores the importance of diversity. This section is incredibly important to understanding why it is critical to encourage new perspectives to enter fields that have long been dominated by men.

PART 1

MINDSET

CHAPTER 1

SO YOU WANT TO HANG WITH THE BOYS

———

"One of the most courageous things you can do is identify yourself, know who you are, what you believe in and where you want to go."

—SHEILA MURRAY BETHEL, CEO BETHEL LEADERSHIP INSTITUTE AND BESTSELLING AUTHOR

* * *

So you want to hang with boys? Maybe you are looking to join a boy's sports team, a Robotics team, a male-dominated career, or some other activity where you might be surrounded by dudes.

Going into a situation like this can be extremely intimidating! As someone who grew up doing martial arts, I can fully understand the guts and hard work that it takes to be successful when you are surrounded by guys.

I am not going to lie to you. Being the only girl is not going to be easy. There are going to be situations that frustrate you. There are going to be situations that are really upsetting. There are going to be times where you wish you had said or done something differently. There will be times that you should have called the boys out on something that they said and you didn't. But you will not regret the amazing feeling of being accepted by a group of guys when you have proven that you are just as good (if not better) than they are!

First things first when you are trying to get involved in any field, but particularly a male-dominated one, do your research! Figure out who has done what you are trying to do before you. If you are a girl who wants to play football, read Becca Longo's story and take a look at Jen Welter's journey. These two women took the football field by storm and both successfully participated in the sport. If you want a job on Wall Street, find a woman who has done it before you.

Looking at the paths of women before you is extremely helpful because it allows you to learn from their mistakes and build on their experiences in order to be successful yourself.

Figure out what obstacles they faced throughout their journeys and create a game plan to help you overcome those obstacles yourself.

Once you find these role models, try to reach out to them. You will be surprised how many women are willing to help other women. Find your role model on Facebook, Instagram, LinkedIn— wherever you can and shoot them a message. The worst case scenario is that they won't respond, so don't be afraid to put yourself out there.

In order to write this book, I had to reach out to countless women across all industries. I received so many kind responses from women who were genuinely excited to get involved in the project. There is no need to be afraid, just think of how you would feel if a younger girl reached out to you asking for your help and advice; odds are you would be flattered!

Below, I am going to show you the method that I used to reach out to the women I wanted to speak to for this book. It worked extremely well for me and you can use it to help find mentors for yourself.

The first thing you want to include in your message, whether you send it through Facebook, Twitter, email, or anywhere else, is an introduction about yourself. Explain who you are and why you are reaching out to this person *specifically*. The key word that I highlighted in that sentence was *specifically*. You want her to feel special and you want to show her you did your homework, similar to how you might prepare before a job interview.

You also need to explain your interest in the field. Why is it something that you want to get into? From where does your interest stem? Have you had any experiences with the field before or are you just getting started?

Next, it is always helpful to include some sort of compliment to your potential mentor. If you are interested in becoming a journalist, cite a piece that was interesting to you written by the person you are looking to contact. If you are interested in comedy, explain how one of her sets inspired you. If this person has written a book, write a review for it on Amazon and mention a part that you enjoyed when you reach out.

If you are struggling to find a compliment, see if you can find some sort of connection to the person. Maybe she is an alumni of your college or maybe you both like the same sports team. Use the internet to help you, tons of information can be found on almost anyone. You just need to show how you are inspired by this person.

Finally, you need a call to action. The easiest thing to ask for is a quick 15 minute phone call. It's not too much of a commitment and it is an easy way to make a first connection. By asking for this call, it gives the person an easy, tangible way to move forward and doesn't leave anything ambiguous.

Here's an example of this method in action. Let's say I want to become a weightlifter. I start by researching female weightlifters online and discover that female weightlifters tend to be big Instagram users. On Instagram, I find a weightlifter named Camille Brown that I am interested in speaking with about her experiences. Here is a sample direct message I could send to her on Instagram:

Hi Camille,
My name is Katie Rogers and I am a junior at Georgetown University. I have been considering getting into weightlifting, but am a little intimidated and don't quite know how to get started. I have been looking through your Instagram account and am extremely inspired by all your hard work, particularly your recent post about failure and how you are overcoming it. I would love to talk to you about your start in weightlifting and hear how you have found so much success. Would you be willing to chat on the phone with me for 15 or 20 minutes?

Best,
Katie

As you can see here, I have all of the successful elements of a compelling message. First, I introduce myself and give a quick background of who I am. Next, I explain my interest in her field. Then, I explain why I am reaching out to her specifically and compliment her on some recent content that she posted. I finish with a question that asks for a response, which makes it more likely that I will hear back from her. Most of all it is short and to the point, so it won't be overwhelming to Camille as she scrolls through her messages.

This method works for any field. Figure out how to best reach your target and reach out with a simple, but meaningful message. You will be shocked at how many women will be willing to respond to you. I reached out to most of the women I spoke with to write this book in this way and they were willing to speak with me and help with my project.

* * *

Once you secure a conversation, you need to know what to ask of your new mentor. Some questions will depend on the field, but below you will find some sample questions that can work for all fields. These questions help you get a sense of what you need to do next in order to get started in the field. Don't limit yourself to these questions, but these are some that I have found to work well and serve as a good foundation for your conversation. Make sure you do research on your role model before speaking with them so that you don't ask them anything you could have found online.

Questions to Ask Your Role Model:

- *Can you tell me how you got started in your field?*
- *Have you had any mentors along the way? How have you been able to build relationships with them?*
- *What obstacles have you faced in this field and how have you overcome them?*
- *What characteristics do you think are important for a woman to have in your field?*
- *What advice would you give to another woman looking to enter your field?*

* * *

After you have talked to a couple of role models, it is time to identify your strengths and weaknesses in terms of your chosen field. What characteristics do you have that will make you successful? What will you need to work on?

Based on your conversations with your role models, you can begin to figure out what you will be good at and what obstacles you might face.

For me, when I began training in martial arts, my biggest obstacle was my physical strength. As a five year old girl, I didn't have much muscle tone, which made it difficult for me in the beginning. Thanks to some encouragement from some awesome instructors (and a little bit of perseverance from a young me), I pushed through this barrier. Over the years I did karate I became very strong as I built the necessary muscles.

When you identify the challenges you might face beforehand, it makes it easier to push through and keep working towards your goals when you encounter these obstacles. If an obstacle is unexpected, it is a lot easier to give up, so try to anticipate the difficulties you could face before actually facing them. Use your mentor(s) to determine potential obstacles and map out what you will do in the face of these challenges.

* * *

Finally, it's time to develop your plan of attack. What is your goal? How are you going to reach it? We will talk more about goal-setting later on in the book, but for now just think about the field you want to enter and what you hope to get out of it.

Becca Longo is a fantastic example of someone who has been able to attack her goals head on. She was the first girl to ever earn a scholarship to a Division II football program. Growing up, she found her interest in football through her older brother. Although separated by an eleven year age gap, they had football in common. They could often be spotted tossing around a football in their backyard and Becca remembers going to all of his games.[6]

Through attending his games, she found her true inspiration to play when she watched a girl by the name of Heidi Garrett set the record for the longest kick from a high school female player. Becca›s brother played on the team with Heidi. When Becca attended a party for the players and their families, she was able to meet her idol. According to Becca, she could not stop staring at Heidi the entire time.[7]

After being inspired by Heidi, Becca expressed her interest in becoming a kicker. She began playing on the football team during her sophomore year of high school and went on to play kicker at Adams State University in Colorado.[8]

In an interview with the LIST SHOW TV, Becca highlighted what she has done in her career as a football player to be successful. First, she emphasizes the importance of hard work. Becca knew that she would need to gain the approval

---

6   "Female Kicker Makes College Football History". 2018. *CNN.* https://www.cnn.com/videos/sports/2017/04/15/female-college-football-kicker-becca-longo-intv-nr.cnn.

7   "Can A Woman Play In The NFL?". 2018. *Sports Feel Good Stories.* https://www.sportsfeelgoodstories.com/can-a-woman-play-in-the-nfl/.

8   Ibid.

of her team. She accomplished this through being the first one on the field and the last one off every day at practice. She would also always do extra sets in the weight room to earn her place on the team.[9] Whether it is fair or not, as a female in a male-dominated environment, you need to put in extra work to prove yourself to the guys around you.

Becca also knew that she would face critics and people who would say offensive things to her. She has been told that she is nothing but a publicity stunt. Becca speaks of the importance of believing in yourself and not listening to anyone who has negative things to say about you.[10] Like former Secretary of State and presidential candidate Hillary Clinton once said "Take criticism seriously, but not personally. If there is truth or merit in the criticism, try to learn from it. Otherwise, let it roll right off you."[11] Surround yourself with positive people who encourage you to be your best and reach your goals, rather than those who will tear you down.

Becca was able to figure out what she needed to do to be successful in football through watching her role models and

9   "Tackle Your Dreams: 3 Tips From Footballer Becca Longo". 2018. *Youtube*. https://www.youtube.com/watch?v=1yrxSzA6OLo.

10 Ibid.

11 Hayes, Martha. 2017. "Hillary Clinton Quotes: The Would-Be President In Her Own Words". *Marie Claire*. https://www.marieclaire.co.uk/entertainment/people/hillary-clinton-quotes-to-make-you-feel-truly-empowered-42730.

working extremely hard. Becca also shows that your role model does not have to be another woman, though it can be helpful to have another woman who may have shared experiences with you. Becca did have Heidi as a female role model, but she also had her brother and coaches as male role models who have helped shape her football career into success. If you are struggling to find a woman in your field that you can relate to, men can also help guide your path.

* * *

The bottom line is do your research and find some potential mentors. Get up the courage to reach out to them and send a simple message detailing who you are and why you want to talk to them. Schedule a quick chat to build a relationship and use the questions above as a foundation for your conversation.

Mentors are often incredibly helpful and we will discuss the role of mentorship more later on. Keep reading to discover how to dominate as a woman in a male-dominated field.

CHAPTER 2

RECOGNIZE THE WORLD ISN'T EQUAL

———

"Be so good at whatever it is that you do that you can't be ignored."

—*FEMALE DIVISION I STRENGTH AND CONDITIONING COACH*

* * *

As you may have realized by this point, the world is not an equal place for everyone. There are different expectations for different people and these differences are largely based on characteristics that we cannot control.

Mary Smith* experienced this when she entered the technology field. When she first made the decision to go into tech it never really occurred to her that it was male-dominated, she just jumped right in.

She got into the industry after a night out at a pub with some of her girlfriends. One of the girl's sisters came in wearing expensive clothing and driving a luxury car and Mary decided that she wanted to do whatever this woman was doing. Luckily for Mary, the woman needed an inside sales representative at the PC supplies company that she was working for. She ended up hiring Mary, which is how Mary started heading down the technology path.

Up to that point, Mary had always been taught that the world is a meritocracy. She had grown up believing the philosophy that everyone has an equal opportunity for success if they worked hard. She took this for granted and assumed that working hard would lead her to success.

It wasn't until she had her first child that she realized the vast gender difference that exists in her workplace. She had to stop working to stay home and care for her colicky baby, while her husband continued going off to work each day.

This was a major cause of anxiety for Mary. She describes this break in career using the analogy of a marathon runner who had been training to race for years. The runner gets to the race, but stops and does nothing for 40 minutes at mile 7. The anxiety that this athlete would face is the same anxiety that Mary faced when putting her career on pause for her family. Just like the men she worked with, she had gone to school, gotten a degree, and worked extremely hard to get to where she was, but was still put at a disadvantage in her career by having children, while those men were not. It is easy to see how women can get behind in their careers due to childbirth, just as a runner would get behind in a race if they had to stop for an extended period of time.

Another issue Mary faced post having children was that people did not take her seriously when she had childcare needs. She found that she wasn't put up for the same promotions as others around her due to her perceived familial obligations.

Once Mary was able to find decent childcare, she began working again part-time on various projects for people in her network. This allowed her to make some money and regain some of her independence, but it created issues for other people's perceptions of her motherhood capabilities. Her mother-in-law told her that she worked too hard and she was not a good mother to her kids because she was working instead of just caring for them. This demonstrates the stigma that still exists regarding mothers going back to work versus staying home with their children.

Mary was surprised by the backlash that she faced. Young women are not prepared for the reality of the constant critiquing of motherhood styles that they will face throughout all of their years of child-rearing. Women are retaliated against for being bad mothers if they go back to work and criticized if they decide to stay-at-home for not being motivated enough to handle a career and a family.

In fact, women are 15% less likely to earn a promotion than men and a woman with children is 50% less likely to earn a promotion than a woman without children.[12] This statistic shows that not only are women discriminated against in the promotion process, but women with children are even more discriminated against than women without children.

Unfortunately, the issue of women losing out on their careers due to childbirth is deeply ingrained in the business world. Many companies are hesitant to hire young women out of fear that they will get pregnant and need to take time off. When you hire a woman and she has a baby, most companies force other employees to cover instead of hiring a temporary employee to take on the woman's responsibilities while she is gone. This creates incredible strain on organizations because

---

12 Nelson, Amy. 2018. "Moms Are Punished In The Workplace, Even When We Own The Business". *The Washington Post*. https://www. washingtonpost.com/news/posteverything/wp/2018/01/29/i-started-my-own-business-i-still-couldnt-escape-stereotypes-about-working-moms/?utm_term=.207bedbe2ba8.

many companies cannot afford to be without an employee for a period of time. Mary relates this phenomenon to playing on a sports team. If your goalie were forced to sit on the sideline and you weren't able to put in a new one, everyone else on the team would have to work harder to cover for the missing player. This creates a hidden reluctance to hire and promote women, particularly in male-dominated fields.

* * *

Julie Magid, a professor at a large university, had similar difficulties when it came to having children in the workplace.

There was one instance when she went for a promotion for a more high profile role at the university. She was passed over for the role and was told that it was because she had small children at home. The role went to a man with kids even younger than hers.

There were many evening social events associated with the role and the assumption was made that she could not handle both the job and her obligations at home. The same assumption was not made for the man who ultimately got the position.

As an employment lawyer, she knew that this decision was illegal. Unfortunately, this conversation was held one-on-one in someone's office, so if she were to have taken legal action, it would have been a he-said, she-said situation. Furthermore, it would have made a bad impression on her ability to be a team player when it came to future promotions and tenure.

She really wanted this position because she felt that it would further her career goal to become a full professor. This was her goal because no woman had ever been promoted from assistant professor to full professor at her particular university campus. Further, there were female full professors that had come from other universities, but many of them were closer to the ends of their careers than Julie, so when they left no female full professors would remain, which would be a detrimental situation for the university's students. It is imperative for students to have exposure to professors who are like them because students are at a disadvantage if they cannot relate to their professors. Furthermore, a diverse faculty brings about a wider variety of ideas and perspectives to help students gain a broader worldview. Hearing different thoughts and beliefs is a critical part of higher education. This applies not only to female professors, but also to professors of different races, sexualities, and backgrounds.

Entrepreneur, Amy Nelson, also experienced something very similar to Professor Magid. While she was working as a corporate litigator, after giving birth to her second child, she asked to be considered for a promotion to an open position within the company for which she worked. Her boss told her that they had "discussed it internally" and that "it wasn't the right time" because she had just had a baby.[13] Amy was stunned by this. She could not believe that her commitment to her job was being questioned because of her status as a mother. At the time, she decided not to report her boss not only out of fear of retaliation, but also because she believed that he was a "good guy."[14] She writes that "even good guys can be wrong."[15] This type of discrimination is extremely worrisome, as it penalizes women with children. No one would ever pass over a man for a promotion because he had children. Why, then, would women be punished for the same thing?

* * *

As you can tell from these women's stories, workplaces are not equal between men and women. There are different expectations between genders, particularly for women with kids. There are also other ways in which women are discriminated against in the workplace, in addition to being held back for having children. These other forms of discrimination ensure

---

13 Nelson, Amy. 2018. "Moms Are Punished In The Workplace, Even When We Own The Business". *The Washington Post*.
14 Ibid.
15 Ibid.

that women typically have to work harder than men do in order to advance their careers and get noticed.

Like Becca Longo's story of needing to work harder than the boys to earn their respect, I had a similar experience in my martial arts training. I always felt as though I needed to work harder than the boys so that I could prove I was just as good as they were. I was always at my karate school and went to every class that was available to me. In class, I consistently put forth my best effort, even when the boys slacked or goofed off. I even took to practicing at home; sometimes alone and sometimes with my sister, who was also training with me.

Feeling like you need to work harder than the boys to earn the same respect that they automatically receive is extremely frustrating, but it is a reality for women in male-dominated environments. The best action you can take in these situations is to work hard and use the need for respect as motivation to improve.

* * *

Emily White*, a strength and conditioning coach at a major university, uses the men around her as her motivation to get stronger. She grew up around boys and to this day if she is going to strength train with someone, it is usually a guy. She says this is just what she is used to and it fits her personality better. She enjoys training with people who are stronger than her because it pushes her to levels that she otherwise would never have thought herself capable.

She doesn't shy away from training with guys and over time she has found this has made her extremely good at pushing herself mentally. In many cases, better than the guys. This has earned her a great deal of respect from male colleagues and counterparts.

She also has other areas that she is better at than the guys, which helps her to gain acceptance. Being smaller and lighter, she wasn't able to squat as much as her big, male football friends, but she was able to beat them at pull-ups. She could do the same with shuttles. She found that playing to her strengths in areas where she could hold her own or even perform better than the guys forced them to respect her. She learned to choose her battles to help her gain instant prestige among the men in the gym.

When she found areas in which she could outperform the men, her male coach would trash talk the guys about how she was beating them and she would begin trash talking them too. Establishing this banter helped her to become a part of the crew and to be perceived as one of the boys.

Throughout her life Emily has learned that strategically finding ways to stand out forces people to respect you. To this day, there are record boards where Emily still stands as the top female record holder in every category. She is a legend.

* * *

If you do stand out, you might find that people will put you down. This is because they are jealous of you, not because they do not respect you. This is an important distinction to understand.

While the world is not equal for men and women, particularly for women working in male-dominated fields, women who turn this disadvantage into an advantage are the ones who are most successful. Use other people's doubts about your abilities to fuel your progress.

*name changed

CHAPTER 3

FIND YOUR PASSION

"Find what you are passion about. Don't let anyone dissuade you from it."

—LISA MASCOLO, EXECUTIVE AT IBM

* * *

The key to making it in an unequal world is finding what you are passionate about and sticking with it.

Camille Brown was a softball player who dreamed of playing softball in a Division I program in college. Her coaches and teammates told her that she wouldn't be able succeed because she wasn't good enough. She was a little scrawny, she didn't run as fast as the other girls on her team, and she couldn't hit the ball out of the infield, but she had a lot of heart and always put in her best effort.

Her dad believed that it would improve her play if she gained some weight and muscle mass, and worked on speed, agility, and form, so he encouraged her to begin strength and conditioning training. She began in a group class at the age of twelve. Of the fifteen participants in the class, she was the only girl. This was extremely intimidating for Camille.

Luckily, she had some awesome, extremely welcoming coaches, including a female coach, but she was still terrified at the beginning of her training.

She ended up becoming extremely competitive with the guys. In the beginning, they would beat her in everything, which was difficult for her to handle. This ultimately drove her to improve. She used the fact that they were better than she was to motivate herself to train hard and become just as good as they were.

By the time she was a senior, she was outperforming most of the guys she had trained with over the past four years. She proved she was a badass who deserved their respect, and she certainly got it. Camille was at the point where she was even sharing barbells with some of the guys and beating them on conditioning drills.

While her strength training was frustrating in the beginning, it ultimately built up her confidence and helped her to build relationships with the guys with whom she trained. They ended up seeing her as a peer because they respected her work ethic and saw that she wasn't joking around.

Now she is accepted in the gym as an equal. Around the gym there are the notorious head nods that guys usually receive from other guys if they are really ripped. Camille gets this head nod too. She also gets a flex and an extra scoop of meat when she goes to Chipotle from the chef in the back of the restaurant.

Through her experiences, she has gained so much confidence. She loves the challenge of pushing herself to add more weight to her lifts. She loves being in an environment that fosters her goals. Most importantly, she loves that she was able to reach her goal of playing collegiate softball. She ended up playing Division I softball at California Polytechnic State University and is now a national Olympic weightlifter and strength trainer, where she helps others achieve their weight-lifting goals.

* * *

Lisa Mascolo, an executive at IBM, also emphasizes the importance of passion to success. She refers to passion as "the fuel for the fight." If you are not passionate about what you do, it won't be fun, it will be too hard, and you won't succeed at it.

Lisa's passion is the public service sector. Her clients have always been governments. Her true passion lies in serving her clients' clients—citizens, benefit recipients, war fighters, taxpayers, students, immigrants, refugees. She gets out of bed each day in order to help government better serve its constituents. Having found and pursued her passion, the work is always enjoyable and rewarding, and the path easier regardless of the environment.

While some come by their passions naturally, Lisa believes that we should actively work to develop skills, the idea of commitment to a cause, and a passion for hard work and the outcomes associated with it in young people, especially young girls. In a world where there are still obstacles for women and young girls, being passionate about what they can do and the difference they can make provides the strength to succeed regardless of obstacles.

* * *

Growing up, Emily, the strength and conditioning coach from earlier in the book, had an older brother and always tried to fit in with him and his friends. She constantly wanted to play outside with them. Because they were older and bigger and because they are boys and she is a girl, she discovered herself in survival mode. Either she needed to keep up with them so she could play and hang out with them or she couldn't keep up and they would ditch her. She kept up. They played all sorts of sports and games together. She also played youth basketball in the boys league until she reached an age where they mandated that she could no longer play with the boys.

Emily fell in love with strength and conditioning in high school. She blew out her knee when she was fourteen in a slide tackle in a soccer game. At the boarding school she attended, she was well connected to the athletic trainers. Her dad recommend that she start working with them, so during the summer following her injury she enrolled in a strength and conditioning camp. She was reluctant to join and only decided to do it because of her dad's urging. The last thing she wanted was to spend her summer running, lifting weights, and being told what to do by a trainer. She ended up participating in the camp, albeit very begrudgingly.

She loved it. She was good at it.

Her training at this camp was with all guys, mostly football players. All of the boys were extremely competitive in training. As she got more and more into her training, Emily could see it transforming her body and drastically improving her performance as a player, so she began attending the camp every summer to train for her Division I soccer career.

She found her two best high school friends during this experience. Both were football players who she did strength training with during the summers. While they lifted together, the boys never wanted to do the conditioning that Emily did for soccer, so she often did that on her own.

She trained with the same trainer through college and he offered her the opportunity to intern with him. In exchange for her work, he allowed her to choose a training session to attend for free. She selected the evening session with the football boys. She worked for the trainer during the day and then trained with the guys at night.

During her junior year of college, Emily suffered a career-ending neck injury. She decided that if she could no longer be an athlete herself, she wanted to train athletes.

After establishing her career goal, she researched what would help her get there. She finished her undergraduate business degree and continued working for the trainer. He suggested that she should go to graduate school to study strength and conditioning. Emily decided that she was only interested in attending the school that her dad had attended. She researched the program and only applied there. She decided that if she got in it was meant to be and if she did not get in she was meant for something else.

She ended up getting into her choice graduate program and obtained her masters in strength and conditioning over a period of two and half years. In her last year and a half in the program she was training four different teams at the school to help her pay off her schooling. She also completed the required internships in both the private and collegiate sectors.

Her advisor got a phone call saying that there was an opportunity open at a university looking to fill the position with a female trainer. Emily and one other woman applied. Emily was fortunate enough to get the position, so she left school early to start her strength and conditioning career. Following her job at this university, she moved on to one more position for six months before getting the call for her current position as a collegiate strength and conditioning coach at an athletic powerhouse.

She initially wasn't interested in moving across the country to take this role, but she realized that if she didn't accept this opportunity at a top ten collegiate program as a 25 year old, she was never going to see another opportunity like this again, so she packed all of her belongings up into her car and traveled across the country to take on this new job. Five and half years later she is still there.

While she has achieved great success in her career and has worked extremely hard, Emily still sees a gender bias in her field. Salaries are not great for strength and conditioning coaches outside of football programs, an area that men tend to gravitate towards. Emily sometimes wonders if she would make more if she were a male, as she might be more interested and accepted in the football programs. Even though she sometimes thinks about this, she has decided that she likes her current position much more than she would like working within a football program. If she were to work in football, she wouldn't get to be in charge, she would be the assistant. She takes great pride in her work and enjoys the influence that she has in her current role.

Emily emphasizes the importance of figuring out your goal and vision for your career. Once you decide on a goal, do not let anyone tell you otherwise. She says to "Find your passion and pursue it relentlessly with all of your heart." Once you decide on your goal, do not give up on it! Determine what you need to do and get after it.

Once Emily decided that she wanted to train athletes, she determined that the best path for her to take was to obtain her master's degree. This degree has given her credibility in her field, which acts as an automatic foot in the door. It is not required for her industry, but it makes it hard for potential employers to overlook her. Make yourself as credible as possible in your chosen field so that you can attract the attention of the organizations where you want to work.

Once you get that job, be diligent and work hard to climb the ladder. Nothing replaces working hard when you are looking for success in your job. Challenges and adversity are part of the process, so do not be afraid when you struggle. Tackle the challenge with everything that you have.

* * *

Hannah von Oldenburg, a manufacturing engineer, found her passion in science. Growing up with three sisters, Hannah was not raised in a particularly male-dominated environment like many other women in male-dominated fields have been. As a triplet, she and her sisters each wanted to have their own identities because they were often compared to one another growing up.

Hannah chose to dive into her math and science classes. This really became her niche, as she ended up joining the robotics team at her high school as one of the only female members. However, being one of the few girls did not faze her. She thought of her teammates as her brothers and ended up realizing the impact and power of engineering. As one of the few girls, she felt like she had the opportunity to try to make the point that she was present, had contributions to make, and that her contributions were as important as any from her male teammates.

Her teachers in high school took notice that there were not many female participants and made an extra effort to provide her with opportunities, made sure that she felt comfortable, and exposed her to problem solving with engineering concepts. They focused on allowing Hannah to succeed as an engineer without her feeling self-conscious about being one of the only girls on the team.

After this first experience with robotics, as a junior in high school, Hannah took an internship at a major oceanographic institute. She worked on designing prototypes of underwater robots. She had a fantastic experience and found her work to be fun, but very challenging. This was especially true given that she had only a high school education and did not yet understand many of the basic physics and engineering concepts required for the job.

To describe what the work was like she said "Imagine someone telling you to build something and you have no idea how to build it because you have never done any engineering like that before."

This experience was very different from that of robotics. Robotics was a program built for high schoolers where they give you a kit and a structure of what to do and you work with a team to accomplish the task. Her real-world experience at her internship was definitely not built for a high schooler, as the other interns were all juniors and seniors in college. In this position, she was given a broad task, like designing a prototype that could swim in a fish tank or pool and was expected to bring it back to her boss. There was much less guidance and structure on these projects than on her robotics projects.

While she was working at the oceanographic institute, many of the college interns went to MIT. Her boss had also gone to MIT. She had never heard much about the school, but it piqued her interest after learning about the school from her coworkers. She figured that she liked engineering and MIT is a great place for that, so she considered applying. She visited MIT that summer, applied, and got in several months later.

While she was in college at MIT, Hannah wanted to try everything. She was interested in doing business, going to medical school, becoming a lawyer. You name it, she wanted to try it. She had no idea what she wanted to do and changed her mind practically every semester.

Because she was unsure of the path she wanted to take, it was important to her to make sure that she was not limiting herself. She ended up studying material science and engineering, which is the study of how things are composed and how to manipulate different properties. This was broad enough to give her a range of options after graduating.

She was surprised to find that her classes were often made up of 70-80% women, given that women are not super prevalent in engineering. This helped her to feel like less of a minority in the engineering world.

Hannah really did not face a male-dominated environment in college until she worked at her internships. She found that in the real-world the statistics were much more representative of the number of women graduating from engineering programs. Spoiler: it's low.

She took on a variety of internships, including one at a major oil and gas company and another doing biomaterial design for cancer patients at a clinical trial group. Toward the end of her MIT career, Hannah took a semester off from school to go work for an aerospace manufacturer as a materials intern. She loved her job so much that she was slightly disappointed when weekends came and she wasn't able to go into work. She was one of the few women in her intern class, but she made friends with several people on the job.

After finishing up her internship, she went back to MIT to complete her degree. She ended up coming back to a similar position in the same aerospace group and ultimately decided to go full-time with a different team after she graduated.

In her job, there are many days where she is the only woman in the room for meetings. All of her technicians are males. She is their engineer and tells them what to do. Sometimes Hannah feels strange that she is freshly out of college and that she is telling men in their twenties through their fifties what to do, how to do their jobs, and how to process things correctly.

Even though Hannah has found herself consistently surrounded by men, she has been motivated throughout her career because loves what she does.

Once you find what you are passionate about, like Camille, Lisa, Emily, and Hannah, it is imperative to set goals. You need to figure out what you want to do and then create a plan for how to get there.

* * *

I started training in martial arts at the age of five. I quickly fell in love with the sport and had my eye on earning my black belt. This is an extremely long-term goal for a little kid. Even people who are unfamiliar with martial arts know that getting a black belt is a huge achievement and takes a ton of time. Luckily, the way martial arts is structured, there are many small milestones on your way to black belt that help keep you motivated and engaged. Instead of constantly focusing on just getting my black belt, I could just focus on working my way up the through all the different colored belts. When I started as a white belt, I focused on earning my yellow belt. Once I had reached that goal, I had my heart set on earning my orange belt. Instead of thinking about how long it would take and how difficult it would be to earn my black belt years and years down the line, I used these smaller goals to make my huge goal much more attainable.

This concept can be applied to any career path. As we have seen, it is especially important for women in male-dominated environments to set goals— and it can be a lot more challenging to stick to them due to obstacles faced in the workplace. Once you decide on a your passion and your goal, break it up into something smaller. If your goal is to be a strength and conditioning coach for a Division I athletic program like Emily, start by getting a job assisting a trainer and look into getting a degree in strength and conditioning, just like she did. These smaller, more tangible steps set you up on a path to success in achieving that ultimate goal.

* * *

As you can see, passion is incredibly important for success. It is also important to realize that it is perfectly fine if you haven't yet found your passion. Some people know really early on what they love and others take a little longer. Do not stress yourself out if you don't know what you are passionate about. And certainly do not just pick something so that you can say you have found your passion.

If you know what you are passionate about, go for it! If not, try new things so that you may discover it. Take classes that sound interesting to you. Talk to people you feel have interesting jobs or hobbies. Try as many new and different things as you can.

PART 2

ACTIONS

CHAPTER 4

BE CONFIDENT

"I've always considered myself the best and the top. I never considered that I was out of it."

—SERENA WILLIAMS, PRO TENNIS PLAYER

* * *

If you want people to take you seriously, particularly as a woman surrounded by men, you need confidence in yourself and in your abilities. If you are not confident, it will be extremely apparent to those around you, making it challenging, if not impossible to earn their respect.

Rachel grew up wanting to be an astronaut. As a child, she was always interested in science. After taking physics in high school, she found that she really enjoyed the problem solving aspect of it. She loves that it is very cut and dry whether or not you get a problem correct. This passion for science has led her to the physics department at Georgetown University. In the senior class of physics majors, of which Rachel is a part, there are around 25 students. Of these 25, about one quarter are women. Last year's graduating class consisted of 15 students and only one was a woman. Clearly, this is a very male-dominated major.

Rachel has become accustomed to this dynamic because she has been surrounded by guys in her program since her freshman year. While she is generally able to fit in with the guys, as she grew up with brothers and always has had more male friends than female friends, she has found that there are some differences between the guys and girls in the group.

In class, she has found that girls, herself included, are less likely to raise their hands than the boys. The guys in the class are willing to raise their hands and throw out an answer, even if they are unsure whether or not they are right. The boy that sits behind Rachel in class will raise his hand to answer a question, get the answer wrong, and then raise his hand again two minutes later to try to answer another question. Rachel finds it much harder to convince herself to raise her hand in the first place. If she does get the courage to raise her hand and answer a question and she gets it wrong, she is likely to be embarrassed and is less likely to speak up in class for the next couple days, whereas the guys are willing to jump right back in. Luckily, professors tend to notice this issue. They sometimes specifically call on female students to involve them in class to ensure that they feel more comfortable speaking up.

Outside of class, Rachel spends quite a bit of time with her male classmates. She enjoys hanging out with them socially, but finds that she does get treated differently from the guys in some ways. For example, her male friends have a constant running joke that she can't drink as much as they can. They will make comments like "Rachel's had half a beer, we better cut her off." While these comments are not meant maliciously, they do highlight that the guys see Rachel's ability to hang with them differently than they do with other guys.

Rachel has found that she must be willing to stand her ground and stick up for herself when necessary. She has also learned that she needs to act with more confidence in class like the guys, and that she shouldn't second guess herself as much. The men in her program tend to be pretty confident when applying for jobs, raising their hands, and asking for research positions, regardless of their qualifications. She tries to emulate this behavior and constantly reminds herself that she is doing just as well or better than most of these guys in class. If they are qualified for a position, so is she.

This confidence has helped Rachel excel in her program. She has learned how to be confident through watching the actions of her male peers. Boys are generally socialized to speak up, whereas girls tend to have a harder time doing so. Through watching and imitating her peers, she has been able to step out of her comfort zone and act more confident in her classes and in searching for jobs. This confidence will help carry her through her career in science, which will likely continue to be male-dominated.

* * *

Marina is the only woman on the team of a bunch of guys at Sunniva, a beverage startup in Washington, D.C. that makes healthy bottled coffee beverages.

After taking a corporate internship and deciding that the corporate world wasn't for her, she realized she wanted to do something less predictable and more fun. She happened to have gone to college with one of the three brothers who founded Sunniva. She called up her college friend who was working on his startup and let him know that she wanted to join his team. She became the first and only female hire in the group of guys.

Marina was comfortable being on this team. Having grown up with an older brother, she was more used to being around men than women. She was always around her brother's friends, playing sports with them, and participating in activities with them, so she has found that being on a team with men is more comfortable for her than being on a team of women.

She also was very involved in organized sports growing up, which introduced her to many guy friends. She has found that many female athletes she has competed against have similar traits to guys in the workplace, so this has helped her immensely when it comes to fitting in with the guys at work.

Her athleticism has given her a lot of credibility with the men on her team. It has allowed her to feel like one of them, as they are all pretty athletic themselves.

She loves all of the men on her team and has found that they have treated her with more respect than some female bosses under whom she has worked.

While the team that she works with is wonderful, she has discovered that the beverage industry as a whole is very male-dominated. The marketing work that Marina does on social media is female-dominated, but the sales areas are very male-dominated.

The guys on her team are cognizant of this and have been very supportive of Marina by encouraging her to act assertively in these scenarios. The coffee drinks that she sells are considered more masculine, so she has to prove herself as having credibility when telling vendors what they should purchase. When she goes into meetings with the guys, they have already built relationships with the men, so it is often challenging for her to build new relationships as a woman.

Marina learned that gaining respect from men in the industry really comes down to how you carry yourself. You need to possess confidence in yourself and your abilities. It is also important to dress the part. Marina has found that she needs to dress in a way that gives her credibility in a male-dominated industry. For her specifically, she will choose running shoes over boots because that gives her a credibility boost in the more athletic environment in which she works.

She also draws lines when it comes to socializing with her male coworkers. She tries not to go out with them because she feels, especially as the only woman, that it is unprofessional. If anything were to happen, it would be detrimental to the team, so she tends to avoid these situations. She also tries not to talk about relationships and other personal subjects with them because, while they are her friends, at the end of the day, this is her job. She finds that it is different for her to speak with the guys about her personal life than it is for guys to talk among themselves, so she avoids doing so. She does socialize with them, but she keeps her distance. If she weren't working with them, she would love to go out with them, but the company comes first.

While she doesn't socialize with the guys very much, they are very good about including her. They always invite her to events and include her in conversations.

Marina believes it is helpful to think of her coworkers as teammates, regardless of whether they are men or women. This helps everyone remain a supportive, cohesive unit. While she acknowledges that you aren't going to like everyone and everyone is not going to like you, it is important to have compassion and respect for other people, regardless of who they are or where they are coming from. You never know what others are going through, so in order to succeed, it is important to give others the respect that you desire for yourself.

Marina also emphasizes the importance of having a lot of confidence. Figure out who you are and own it. That is how you earn respect. Don't try to be someone that you are not, because no one likes fake people.

Always be receptive to criticism. Sports prepared Marina to accept criticisms gracefully. Criticism allows you to learn and grow as a person from your mistakes. Always ask yourself "How can I do it better next time?" Don't allow criticism to damage your confidence, rather use it to improve your performance going forward.

* * *

Being confident is important to your success in any industry, but particularly so in male-dominated ones. Men tend to be much more outspoken than women in the workplace so be sure to speak up and ensure that you are heard. Don't live in fear of saying something wrong. If you do, it is not a big deal. Everyone makes mistakes and it is far better to put yourself out there than to stay silent.

A female CEO once told me that because she gets interrupted so frequently by men in her industry, she has learned not to be afraid of telling them that she is not done speaking. Assert yourself, especially when you have the knowledge and expertise to contribute.

CHAPTER 5

STAND UP FOR YOURSELF

"Each time a woman stands up for herself, without knowing it possibly, without claiming it, she stands up for all women."

—MAYA ANGELOU, WRITER AND ACTIVIST

* * *

Don't be afraid to speak up when you are being treated unfairly. That being said, you need to choose your battles.

Julie, a business professor at a major university, emphasizes the importance of knowing your value. One issue that she adamantly speaks out for is the issue of pay. More often than not, she is willing to go on the record stating her beliefs about pay when she feels it is unjust. She believes that on this issue she simply owes it to every single person who works with her. It is not just women who are impacted by differences in pay, but also families. Because this issue impacts everyone, she makes it one of her top priorities.

Julie knows that she has not been paid equally throughout her career. She began her law career at the same firm as her husband and did similar work as him during her time there, and therefore knew that there were pay discrepancies between men and women for equal work. Now that she works for a public university, salaries are public information, so she can see what others earn. She feels that because everyone can see salaries, she is doing a disservice to others if she doesn't say anything to try to make the world more equal.

The Equal Pay Act requires that men and women be paid the same for doing the same job. The way that the law is written, however, allows employers to differentiate pay based on other factors, such as differing degrees and time taken off from work. Basically, if the employer can come up with any reason other than sex to pay someone differently, then it can be legal. This makes proving discrimination an extremely challenging battle to fight, as employers only need to prove that gender is not the basis for their compensation decisions.

At her public university, degree determines salary. There is no reflection of responsibilities or the amount of research published. All that matters is a faculty member's degree. A Ph.D. in Finance, for example, gets paid more than a J.D. This effectively works as a gender bias, as most people with Ph.D.'s in Finance are white males, whereas J.D.s have a more even split between genders.

When negotiating pay, the university will tell its faculty to go get an offer from another university if they want to discuss pay increases. This method is problematic because the academic community is small and you are burning bridges if you go through the hiring process at one university just to get an offer at another for your own personal gain.

Pay inequality is much easier to approach than something like promotion decisions, as pay is much more clear cut. Particularly in Julie's case, there is evidence showing how much she earns versus other people. It is far more objective than deciding whom to promote. It is also a subject in which Julie is an expert. She can say "I know what I am talking about here," and be confident in the case she is making. She points out that if you go after an injustice not in your area of expertise, you put yourself more at risk. This is why she chooses her battles carefully. It is easy to want to fight every injustice that you see, but you need to pick the most important issues to you, rather than fighting for all of them.

Think through when you decide to speak your mind about subjects pertaining to your personal promotion and career growth but don't fear making sure that you are heard and giving your insights in the work setting. You are in your job for a reason. They did not hire you to be a seat-filler and a "yes" person. You were hired to bring your perspectives and insights, so make it count, otherwise you are not doing a good job with the seat you are in.

When determining whether to speak out about an issue, you need to figure out what is important to you and where you can potentially make a difference. It is a balancing act.

* * *

Mary Smith, the executive in the tech industry mentioned earlier, also has experienced mistreatment throughout her career. She once asked her boss for a promotion, as she wanted the opportunity to make connections with the new female executives at a company with which Mary's company worked. She had worked extremely hard for five years at her company. Her boss would make jokes about her promotion, but he did not believe it was important for her to make connections with these new female leaders. He thought that they would not last in their roles.

As it turned out, these women that Mary wanted to network with did remain in their positions. In fact, they became even stronger and Mary was able to have great access to them. Unlike the old leadership, these women wouldn't cave to her boss. He started becoming extremely frustrated with them and would call them bitchy. In her retort Mary explained that they were just really good businesspeople and that they were no longer letting Mary's company take advantage of them.

Mary's boss really resented her relationship with these strong women but took a liking to Mary's counterpart at this other company, who was a man named Peter*, and began treating him somewhat like a son. They built a strong, masculine relationship that Mary could not have had with her boss because it would have been inappropriate and unprofessional.

Peter would often take credit for getting hard things done and would receive praise and admiration from Mary's boss, even though he was not actually responsible for the accomplishments. Mary became fed up with this behavior and set up a meeting with her boss and the CFO at the other company, who she was really good friends with and who knew the true story of Peter's "accomplishments." The CFO explained to Mary's boss what really happened and proved that it was not Peter's doing, even though he had taken credit for it.

Peter ultimately heard about this meeting and grew extremely angry. One night when they were out celebrating with clients Peter suggested that they go to a bar before the events of the evening. The bar he brought them to was a strip club. It was a blatant play by Peter to get Mary out of his way.

It is unbelievable that this event occurred just two years ago. Women are still facing these ridiculous situations. When these incidents occur, there really is no way to win. Mary points out the challenges of these situations. It is inappropriate and unprofessional for her to attend a strip bar, but it is also hard to complain about these things because some might label her a whiner.

This story did find its way back to the women on the leadership team at Peter's company, and he was out of his job within six months. This angered Mary's boss, as he had taken Peter under his wing. He began telling Mary that she did not need to come to big company events and would instead invite Peter. This tension started to affect her health and ultimately Mary left the company after deciding that she could not work well in this environment.

* * *

Hannah von Oldenburg is a manufacturing engineer. She, too, has needed to stand up for herself on occasion in her male-dominated workplace. While she has had good experiences with many coworkers, she still faces sexism. In fact, she says that sexist things have happened to her at most of the companies where she has worked. After an incident occurs, when she gets home she will think "Was that thing that person said right? Should they have said that to me?"

One example of sexism she faced was in a prior position she held. Hannah met with a male mentor for lunch and asked him how he plans for his future in the hopes that he could offer her some guidance for her own path. He told her that the way for her to get ahead in her career was to marry the right man. This is something that would never be said to a male mentee, yet this man thought it was appropriate for Hannah as a female engineer. At the time, Hannah was very young and was unprepared to stand up for herself in that situation.

Hannah has gotten better at processing sexist moments and has grown more assertive in dealing with them. She is less afraid to speak up for herself and will say something like "I don't think what you just said was right" to someone who says something inappropriate to her. She has found herself better equipped to call people out when she feels that they are being unfair.

Many of the other engineers she works with have inherent biases against women. For example, she faces the challenge of working with older engineers who have not worked with female engineers before. Luckily, her current company has a very young, progressive, accepting culture. Most people do not care what you look like, what religion you practice, or where you grew up. They really just care about how you perform and what output you provide for the organization.

Hannah has had both good and bad experiences as a female engineer, but overall she has found her career to be extremely rewarding. She emphasizes the importance of not being afraid to stand out. She says "You might be the only female in the room, but that does not mean it is a bad thing to stand out." This is a powerful image for women entering her field.

She also says to dress the way you want to dress and to be confident in yourself. It is important not to worry about what others think of you and how your contributions will impact what they think. Just be yourself and you will go far.

* * *

Madeline, a salesperson at a computer software company, has also discovered the importance of sticking up for herself in the workplace. Once she worked extremely hard for a promotion against a number of her male coworkers. When she earned the position, someone told all of the male candidates that she must have only succeeded through sleeping with someone and that she "leveraged her feminine guiles to get it."

This experience was extremely disheartening for Madeline, as she had worked very hard to earn the position and these people at her company were acting as though she hadn't truly deserved it.

One thing that her team and organization as a whole have been working on is creating a culture where everyone feels included and welcome. They have acknowledged that diversity is important and have been really good about hiring more women and minorities. Madeline believes this has great benefits because it brings much more diversity to the sales floor. People who might have felt excluded or disenfranchised in the past feel more empowered to succeed in their roles.

Still, she says there is a little bit of a boys club gap when working largely with males. She was friends with many boys in high school, so she has learned how to deal with guys and compensate for this gap. She says it is important that women are not afraid to call guys out when they say things that are inappropriate or don't sit well with her. Once, she had a coworker who she did not know very well put his hand on her shoulder at a work event. She responded, saying to the man "You need to take your hand off my shoulder." She expressly called him out for behavior that was unacceptable and unprofessional. She emphasizes the importance of letting people know that you have boundaries and that they need to respect them, as she did in this case with her coworker who touched her without her consent.

One pervasive problem in sales is that there are constant jokes that saleswomen should flirt with their customers in order to increase sales. At Madeline's company, they are working to cut out that perception. They emphasize that just like the male salespeople, the women are having professional calls with their customers. Saying that they should flirt to make sales is offensive and implies that they are not as good as the men.

Madeline has been surprised with some of the ways men have acted towards women in the workplace. She says there are some things that you might think people should understand, but they don't. In these situations it is important to communicate clearly about what is acceptable and what isn't. She also notes that fixing this problem is an ongoing process. However, through hiring more women to the sales team, her company has changed the entire culture of the sales floor over the past year. For her, it is extremely cool to watch women being treated much differently than they were only a year ago.

This has happened largely through the college recruiting that her company and many other companies focus on. By attracting younger and more progressive employees from universities who bring their modern views that empower young people, particularly women, to move up, companies have made their cultures more inclusive.

The one thing Madeline has learned from working in a field dominated by men is that if there is an issue, you need to speak up for yourself sooner rather than later. Women need to learn to be more assertive in these roles. It can be harder for women because men are taught to be assertive throughout their lives, while women are taught that assertiveness is not ladylike. Madeline feels that the best way to get better at standing up for yourself is to practice. She knows that it is often uncomfortable and you may not want to step on people's toes, but if you want to advance professionally and find success in your career, you must assert your position and know your value. Men are trained to do so, and you may fall behind if you don't. Learning how to speak up for yourself in your first role is really key to your success in the future.

* * *

Marie Harf's way of standing up for herself was deleting her Twitter account. Marie, who now works as an analyst at Fox News, formerly worked for the State Department and the

CIA. She believes that getting rid of her Twitter account is the healthiest thing she has done for herself.

Marie felt she had no choice but to get rid of her Twitter account when she stepped into the public eye as the State Department's deputy spokesperson because she would get daily rape threats, threats of sexual violence, and other threatening messages. There were memes made about what a stupid sorority girl she was. The language used to criticize her on Twitter was very gendered and age specific.

She says that getting rid of her Twitter account has been extremely healthy. According to Marie "Twitter is a nasty place for women. It is nasty for everyone, but it is especially nasty for women."

She feels as though social media sites do not do enough to protect women in the public eye from harassment, threats, and bullying. She sees no personal benefit from being on these social media sites and she feels that they are not a safe place, particularly for women. She refuses to check these sites, saying "I don't need a platform for people to threaten me."

It is not beneficial for anyone to have people constantly attacking them. Marie doesn't need Twitter in order to have a successful career. Getting her message across on Twitter isn't worth going through all of the harassment she faces, particularly because now she works for Fox News which gets plenty of views without her needing to tell her Twitter followers to watch because "people watch Fox."

When she was a government spokesperson, however, she felt that she needed to use Twitter, as it was a very effective way to communicate. She kept her account until the end of the administration because as a public servant it was a good way to communicate with reporters and the public about the work that they were doing. As a private citizen, however, she feels that the platform is entirely unnecessary for her to use given all of the hate she has received on it.

She mentions that while Twitter can be an extremely bad place for women, it can have its merits in certain circumstances, such as with the #MeToo movement, which used Twitter to spread. Marie believes the movement was empowering for women, particularly those in media or government where a lot of issues have been brought to light. However, Twitter-fueled social movements also feel overwhelming to her in some cases, as the #MeToo movement showed everyone that the problem is worse than anyone thought. "We all thought it was bad, but it is worse than any of us thought. At this point we are not even fighting about equal pay anymore, we are just trying not to get raped at work."

The #MeToo movement showed that as a woman, if you yourself have not experienced sexual harassment or assault, you probably know someone who has. This situation is insane and has not been grappled with until now because men face an entirely different experience. Obviously sexual harassment and assault can happen to anyone, regardless of gender, but the fact of the matter is, while most women have either experienced it themselves or know someone who has, most men probably do not even know of another man who has faced sexual assault or harassment. This is why the movement was so important, as it showed the problem was even more prevalent than anyone could have imagined.

Marie points out that this problem isn't particular to any industry. It is not a conservative problem or a liberal problem. It is an everyone problem.

As a woman, it is hard to find the right balance between fighting back against online trolls and ignoring them. You can only fight so much before you become consumed with it and with how people see you.

Marie thinks that one way to solve this problem is by holding online platforms more accountable for regulating themselves. While she realizes that this is an unpopular position to hold and recognizes the importance of free speech, she believes that if sites like Twitter want to be taken seriously as a place for serious people to interact, they are unacceptable in their current forms.

Similarly, for a long time on Facebook they have provided the option to report a comment as abusive. When you make a report, it provides you with a list of ways the content was abusive for you to choose from. It lists several options but gendered insults is not one of them. Marie complained to them about it at one point because a large portion of online harassment is gender based. She feels that these platforms either need to do better to address these issues or women need to stop using them.

She recognizes that this can be extremely challenging. As someone who gave up Twitter, she understands that it is really addicting. But it is also critical that women protect themselves from harassment and violence online if these platforms will not.

Marie acknowledged that she has been fairly fortunate that issues of sexual harassment have not come up for her too often. She has only faced them at some points in her career, but believes progress is being made and is optimistic that things will continue to improve. The most concerning piece of modern harassment to Marie is what happens online. Not just for gender issues, but for a whole host of issues, though particularly how women are treated. She feels that women who want to be a part of the conversation online should not have to pay the price of being threatened and harassed in order to do so.

If someone disagrees with a man on social media, they may call him stupid or an idiot and that is the end of it. For women, it is so much worse. The harassment is much more threatening and much more sexualized. It is much more aggressive. There is no question at all in Marie's mind that this is the case and she thinks that it is unacceptable. Men have told her she should just avoid reading the comments, but the fact that she knows there are comments out there makes it impossible not to. She also points out that you have to read them in part because some threats might be serious and if there is a real threat you have to know about it.

While one way Marie has stood up for herself is by reducing her online presence, she also has also found ways to stand up for herself outside the internet. When Marie was at a large security conference in Aspen, Colorado two years ago, while she worked for the State Department, a senior CIA official whom she did not know while she worked at the agency, but was also at the conference and came up to meet her. While Marie was at the State Department, she would run secure video conferences on serious counter-terrorism issues, partly because she had worked on those issues at the CIA. This man, who looked to be in his 50s, came up to her and told her that when he saw her leading those meetings, he would put it on mute and say to everyone in the room "Why aren't the CIA spokespeople that attractive?" Then he would talk about how Marie looked about sixteen years old.

When he told her this, Marie was stunned that in a professional setting, talking about such serious topics, someone would say that he had muted her to talk to all of the other CIA officials in the room and made comments about her looks and her age. She just couldn't believe what this person was saying. She so badly wanted the perfect comeback, but she couldn't come up with anything because she was in such disbelief.

"So, I think that's illustrative of the fact that I do look a certain way. I'm female, I'm relatively young and I do have blonde hair. And I do think there were times, particularly when I was a spokesperson at the State Department where I was publicly representing the department that I got a lot of criticism and mockery both online from people I don't know and from colleagues because of my gender and more importantly, my age."

There have definitely been things said about Marie that would not have been said about men in the job or even about older women. Marie says that "Yes, absolutely I was treated differently because I'm a woman both by my colleagues and by the public."

When Marie first had these positions, she believed that because she was smart and knew what she was talking about she could wear her hair however she wanted, or dress the way she wanted, and it wouldn't matter. Unfortunately, she underestimated the effect of these things at first. She realized the real world is not so fair. While she is not sure that she has ever fully learned to cope with this reality, she found that taking a step back to go work for Secretary Kerry behind the scenes for the last two years of the administration gave her a good perspective for when she returned to media on Fox.

When she came back on air, she realized that, unfair as it might be, she needed to become more cognizant of people's perception of her. This realization was difficult because no one wants to believe that people are treating you differently. All of that stuff shouldn't matter, and yet it does. When she thinks back to her earlier roles in the public eye, she asks herself "Would I have been maybe a little less combative? Maybe. Would I have worn different things, looking back on it? Maybe." She is not sure she did a good job with dealing with perceptions at the time. "You just put your head down and you go to work and I think I needed to take a step back and look at it with the benefit of time and space to do better."

While she feels that she should not have to worry about trivial problems like if her hair was too puffy that day and made her look like a ditz and, though it makes her angry that she even has to think about it, she realizes that sometimes these issues can have a major impact and should not be ignored.

The lesson to take from Marie is that if you are experiencing any sort of harassment at work, it is imperative that you take action. There are a variety of ways to handle these situations, but you need to stick up for yourself because you deserve to feel comfortable and safe in your work environment.

* * *

As a woman in a male-dominated field, you need to learn to stand up for yourself. People are not always going to respect you or listen to you. Others will not always treat you fairly. Remember that you are worthy and that you deserve to be there just as much as anyone else does. Fight like hell to prove it.

*name changed

CHAPTER 6

TAKE RISKS AND PERSIST

———

"If they don't give you a seat at the table, bring a folding chair."
—SHIRLEY CHISHOLM, FIRST AFRICAN-AMERICAN
WOMAN ELECTED TO THE U.S. CONGRESS

* * *

Being a woman in a male-dominated field takes work. A lot of work. There will be times when you face challenges or failure. There will be times when people tell you that you can't succeed. It is how you respond in those moments that will define your success.

The key to persistence is refusing to take no for an answer. When someone tells me that I can't do something, my first instinct is to prove to them that I can. When communicating with guys, I like to show my confidence because I have found that this is how they communicate with each other. I tend to talk a big game and claim that I can do anything better than they can. One time after stating that I could beat a boy way taller and bigger than I was in a sparring match, he laughed at me and told me that there was no way. We sparred and I kicked his ass.

While I have been able to prove myself in many circumstances where I claim that I am better than the guys, there are also times I have fallen short. One of my close friends is a guy who does a lot of weightlifting. Even I will admit (grudgingly) that he is much stronger than I am. One time, he jokingly challenged me to an arm wrestle. Knowing that I would lose, I accepted the challenge anyway and put forth a formidable effort. While it is unlikely I will ever beat him outright in an arm wrestle, I was able to show that I was more of a match than he expected, which helped me to earn his respect. I also use these moments to motivate myself to become even better.

* * *

You are never going to achieve your maximum level of success without taking risks. Playing it safe can only get you so far.

Madeline, mentioned in the last chapter, took a risk when she accepted a position at a computer software company. She started in a college recruiting program in a sales role, which was fairly male-dominated. Her first job was in business development where she mainly did lead generation. She worked her way up to a sales executive position. In the business development role, the gender breakdown was dominated by men, but was a much more even split than when she started on the sales floor, which had only three or four women out of a group of 100 or so employees. The extreme gender imbalance was a stark difference from her starting position and she says it was nerve-wracking to go onto the sales floor with so many guys and so few women.

She believes that this is beginning to change. Two years ago it was a whole lot of dudes, but now the company is working to become more diverse. Her group and the organization as a whole, is creating a more inclusive culture where everyone feels welcomed.

She found that particularly when she first started, the guys tended to be better at networking and making calls, and they really just excelled, whereas the few females were more hesitant to ask for things and didn't seem to know how to stand up for themselves. Madeline experienced this challenge personally and found it was, and still is, very difficult for her to overcome. She also was frustrated watching the guys doing better than she was.

Instead of giving up or allowing the status quo to remain, Madeline worked to change the situation. To match the superior performance of her male counterparts, Madeline began watching some of the louder, more outspoken guys in her office and tried to copy their mannerisms and discovered it helped her become more successful. She learned from imitating some of their behaviors that when she stands up for herself like the guys do, people tend to respect her more for it, while that behavior is simply expected from the men.

Madeline didn't give up when she faced obstacles, she kept pushing through. This echoes back to the importance of defining goals and sticking to them. Madeline knew that she could get better and worked until she did. When Madeline went up against eight male coworkers and one other female coworker for a competitive spot on the sales team, she was told by each of the men that they had the position in the bag and that she wasn't going to get it. Instead of losing hope and giving up, Madeline stayed late to put in extra hours and redoubled her effort at work. She spent countless hours preparing and networking and doing all sorts of extra activities to ensure she received the position. She did end up earning the job after all of her hard work.

* * *

There will also be times where you will experience failure. Weightlifter Camille Brown, from earlier in the book, understands firsthand what it is like to fail over and over again. She began weightlifting to help her improve her softball game enough to play at the collegiate level. Camille says that "softball is a game of failure." If you get a hit 3 out of 10 times, you are batting .300 and that is considered a decent batting average. It is constant failure. Because of that, you learn that failure is part of the process. It is all part of growth. If you are not failing, then you are not trying hard enough. This mentality is important because it encourages you to keep going, even if things are not going the way that you want them to.

You might be in a slump. For instance, say you are only getting 2 hits out of every 10 at bats. That's a slump. Everybody goes through it. You can either dwell on a slump or you can work to get out of it. You need to get back to practicing. If you find yourself in a slump, it is important to realize that whatever you are doing is not helping you get out of the slump. They key is figuring out what you can do differently to get out of it and continue improving.

This is true in softball and also in every other aspect of life. There will be times that you hit slumps. Whether it is in school, in your job, or in your personal life, we all face obstacles at some point or another. When you do hit a wall, you need to figure out why whatever it is that you are doing isn't working and how you can change to perform better.

In weightlifting, Camille has had a similar experience with failure. For the snatch and the clean and jerk in Olympic weightlifting, weightlifters get three attempts at each for a total of six lifts. The goal is to lift the most weight over the course of the six lifts. In order for your scores to count, you just need to make one lift of each type. That is 1/3 of the lifts. You only need to make 1/3. It is constant failure. You are going until you fail. You are going until you can't lift up that bar anymore. Going until failure is part of the weight room. This scares people but it shouldn't. In reality, you need failure to see how far you can go. It is how you grow and get stronger.

* * *

You need to learn accept failure and to learn how to take failure and turn it into growth. This is incredibly important for women in male-dominated fields. It is never going to be easy for women in male-dominated fields to find success. You are going to face obstacles and need a willingness to struggle and fail at times in order to succeed.

Don't be afraid to fail. Never let the possibility of failure stop you from taking a risk or trying something new. Certainly do not give up if you fail. Some of the most famous, successful, women have failed many times before they succeeded.

Have you ever read Harry Potter? Whether you have or not, you probably know the name of the woman who wrote it. J.K. Rowling is widely considered one of the most successful authors of all time. From the time that she was a child, Joanne Kathleen Rowling knew that she wanted to write books. By the age of six she had already written her first book, which happened to be about a rabbit named Rabbit. According to Rowling, when her mother praised her for this first book, a young Joanne thought "well, get it published then." She had very clear goals from this very young age.[16]

Rowling did not have an easy childhood, however. Her mother fought a tough battle with multiple sclerosis and died when Rowling was 25 years old. She describes the day her mother died as the "most traumatizing moment of her life."[17]

After her mother's death, Rowling moved to Portugal and started teaching English as a foreign language. There she

16 Gillett, Rachel. 2018. "From Welfare To One Of The World's Wealthiest Women—The Incredible Rags-To-Riches Story Of J.K. Rowling". *Business Insider*. https://www.businessinsider.com/the-rags-to-riches-story-of-jk-rowling-2015-5.

17 Ibid.

met Jorge Arantes, who she ended up marrying and having a daughter with, after suffering a miscarriage. After enduring the rocky marriage for a little over a year, Arantes and Rowling separated. Joanne moved to Edinburgh with her infant daughter and three chapters of writing that would ultimately become Harry Potter.[18]

At this point in her life, Joanne felt helpless. She was a single mother without a job. She had to enroll in a welfare program to support herself and her daughter. She was diagnosed with depression and even contemplated suicide. She described herself saying "I was the biggest failure I knew."[19] Through all of her struggles she did not give up her writing and finished the first book in the Harry Potter series, mostly in cafes with her daughter sleeping next to her as she wrote. She secured an agent to shop her book around to different publishers. She was rejected by twelve different publishers.[20] Twelve.

Many people may have given up at this point. Not Joanne. After receiving rejection after rejection, Joanne's manuscript was finally given the go-ahead by a London publisher called Bloomsbury after it had garnered the approval of a company executive's young daughter. The publisher advised Joanne

---

18 Ibid.
19 Ibid.
20 Ibid.

to get a day job, as she likely wouldn't make much from the book.[21]

The publisher also determined to target young boys with the book, so they suggested that Joanne use initials, as little boys would be less likely to want to write a book written by a woman, which is how the name J.K. Rowling was born. The publisher actually told her that boys wouldn't want to read her book if they knew it was written by a woman.[22] This is an offensive mindset to female writers and definitely something that the writing world needs to work on, but J.K. Rowling did what was necessary to appeal to the group which she was targeting. And, boy did she have appeal.

The books were wildly successful in the UK and in the United States. J.K. Rowling wrote and published seven total books in the series, all of which were made into very successful movies. Her books also had a huge crossover appeal to girls, as well as boys.

J.K. Rowling wrote the book while living off welfare and now the franchise she created is worth tens of billions of dollars.

21 Lawless, John. 2005. "Revealed: The Eight-Year-Old Girl Who Saved Harry Potter". *The New Zealand Herald*. https://www.nzherald.co.nz/lifestyle/news/article.cfm?c_id=6&objectid=10333960.
22 Cueto, Emma. 2014. "What J.K. Rowling Using A Male Pseudonym Says About Sexism In Publishing". *Bustle*. https://www.bustle.com/articles/15839-what-jk-rowling-using-a-male-pseudonym-says-about-sexism-in-publishing.

* * *

I tell the story of J.K. Rowling to show that successful people often experience challenges. What sets successful people apart from people who are not successful is the willingness to take risks and really put in the work necessary to reach their goals. The lesson here is that you should not give in to discouragement if you are struggling to accomplish your goals. J.K. Rowling was rejected TWELVE times before she was picked up by a publisher.

She risked everything to put all of her time into her writing. She pushed through extremely challenging times and really channeled her emotions into a project she believed in.

* * *

Now I am not saying that you need to go into poverty to be successful, but it is critical to take smart risks to achieve your goals. You often need to put your fears aside, whether it is fear of being the only girl, fear of failing, or fear of some other element of your pursuit. Do not let the fears that you have impede your success.

Never give up. The common theme you will see from all of the women in this chapter, as well as all of the women in this book, is that they never gave up. Every single woman in this book has experienced challenges in her life and her career, yet not a single one gave up when things were tough.

Saying that you are willing to take risks and that you won't give up is a lot easier than actually doing so. To make sure you stick to it, someone must hold you accountable. Sometimes it can be challenging to hold yourself accountable, so request help from someone else. Pick a trusted family member, friend, mentor, anyone you know who will actually motivate you to continue down the right path and tell them what you are working to achieve. Having someone else who knows what you want to accomplish makes it much harder for you to give up on yourself.

PART 3

WORDS

CHAPTER 7

BREAK THE LOCKER ROOM

———

"You can't always be the strongest or most talented or most gifted person in the room, but you can be the most competitive."

—PAT SUMMITT, TENNESSEE WOMEN'S
COLLEGE BASKETBALL COACH

* * *

There is nothing quite like a literal men's locker room standing in the way of a woman doing her job. Mary Smith found herself literally in a men's locker room at one point.

Mary Smith never would have expected that her customers would put the moves on her. But they did.

This put her in extremely uncomfortable situations. She would be working in a professional environment, trying to get new business from a big company and the CEO would hit on her. In her experience, it is extremely difficult to build relationships with male clients without putting herself in potentially bad situations. Her male colleagues could take male clients out for drinks in order to build rapport and gain access. Mary couldn't do this same thing out of fear of her client taking it the wrong way.

When Mary raised this issue to her male team, they were completely oblivious to what she had been experiencing, as they had never faced those issues. She asked them to not leave her alone with male clients in those situations. Always having a wingman was extremely important to ensure that Mary could feel comfortable while doing her job.

This is a huge barrier women face in male-dominated fields. They are unable to have the same relationships with male coworkers and clients that their male counterparts can. This is often detrimental to their ability to do their jobs well.

In one case, Mary took a group of male clients to a golf outing at a course in Florida. The guys all went out to play golf, while Mary waited for them to come back for a business dinner. They were running late and Mary was scrambling to figure out where they were. It turned out that the men she was supposed to be wining and dining in order to get their business were in the men's locker room bar with a famous golfer. These men literally were in the locker room, while the woman they had come with (and who was paying the tab for the entire trip) was waiting on them to come to dinner.

Ultimately, Mary decided that because she was paying for the outing, she deserved to have access to her clients, so the famous golfer escorted her into the men's locker room.

This is similar to female sportscasters who struggle to gain access to the action in men's locker rooms. This is an issue for women across fields.

Mary was outraged by this occurrence. She should never have been excluded from interacting with her clients in this way. However, when she tells others this story, most are not nearly as outraged as she is. In fact, a common reaction to this story is laughter over how funny it is.

In reality, these situations are not funny. They are extremely limiting to women in male-dominated fields. How can women expect to hang with the men when they are excluded from the very rooms where men are spending their time?

This is why it is imperative to insert more diversity into work-places that are heavily dominated by men. Diversity brings different perspectives and helps those who are different from one another feel included. Diversity breeds understanding for the perspectives of those who may face different adversities, and provides a more open and inclusive atmosphere in and out of the workplace.

* * *

Another obstacle women face in workplaces dominated by men is social inclusivity. Lynn Hurley, who works in con-struction, finds that while the "good old boys network" is not nearly as bad as it used to be, it is still present. The guys she works with often like to get together after work or on week-ends to socialize, sometimes playing golf or going fishing. There is a natural separation between the activities that men are perceived to enjoy and the activities women are perceived to generally prefer, which can create a social barrier between the genders. Furthermore, the men do not typically think to include the women in these social gatherings. Typically this is not intentional, rather they just do not even think about inviting the woman or realize the consequences that can result from the social exclusion of women in male-dominated environments. For example, if male coworkers are spend-ing time together outside of work and they start discussing their jobs or the company, they may reveal information or informally make decisions. If women are never invited, they are entirely left out of these conversations.

Lynn notes that it is totally fine if men want to spend time with just the boys sometimes, but it is important that women are included socially, as it helps foster a better work environment and also makes sure that everyone is on the same page.

While there is a social barrier between men and women, there are activities that can cross over. For example, Lynn says that they can all go drink beer together, which is never a problem. Drinking appears to transcend gender. Everyone loves to grab a drink after a long day of work.

* * *

Professor Julie Magid has faced many obstacles in the networking arena, both as a woman and as someone who didn't come from a privileged background. She lived on a farm growing up and did not have any family connections in business or law. She was lucky enough to attend an elite university that provided her with some great networking opportunities with the people she met, but it did not really occur to her to begin networking until after she graduated from her undergraduate program. She didn't understand that connections are really what drive the professional world.

It is challenging for Julie, and many women in traditionally male-dominated fields, to take advantage of networking and get the same opportunities that men do. At the first law firm she worked at after graduating from law school, the entire law firm would gather in the basement of their building on Fridays at five o'clock and drink beer together. This provided all employees with the same opportunities to network and talk with one another. Julie didn't realize that this was not the norm until she went to a firm that didn't provide this opportunity to socialize. At companies that do not encourage activities like this, the guys have traditions of going out on Fridays or playing games of pick-up basketball while the women are not included.

There are also many men in the business world who ascribe to the Mike Pence philosophy of not inviting women out, not interacting one-on-one with them, or not including women unless spouses are involved. This really creates a barrier for women, as men do not think twice about socializing with other men, but often refuse to treat women in the same way. This means that women have to really impress others with the work that they do, which forces them to keep taking on more and more work. This becomes a self-fulfilling prophecy, because as they take on more work it becomes more difficult to find time to network.

This is still something that Julie finds herself struggling with, even after being in a professional environment for many years. She has established that she does not golf and is not going to start. For a lot of people, when they find that they are left out of a networking opportunity, they will try and take part in whatever the guys are doing, so if the guys are golfing, the woman will learn to golf. This has never been Julie's approach. She feels that even if she were to learn to golf, women are treated differently on the golf course than men because it is such a traditionally gendered activity.

The best way Julie has learned to handle this networking barrier is to find other, more inclusive ways to network outside the office. She finds people who all have tickets to the theater and gets them together to go on the same night. She will invite people to dinner and make connections with them that way.

She also enjoys drinking, which is one commonality she shares with many men. Julie would struggle even more with networking if she didn't drink because that is one activity that acts as bridge between her and male coworkers. She, for example, is the only woman on her floor who is included in the occasional Friday beer after work with the guys because they have realized that she can keep up with them. While this is a connection she can make, she acknowledges that this is not necessarily the best or healthiest networking method.

She also often feels like she needs to go because if she starts saying no, they will stop asking her to come, which will further limit networking opportunities.

She also recommends that if a female feels excluded from an activity that male coworkers are taking part in to say in a positive, non-threatening way "Hey, I wanna do that!" It is important not to let fear stop you from putting yourself out there, otherwise you may not get those opportunities. Oftentimes, men aren't excluding women purposefully, they just don't even think about how their actions might limit female involvement.

Women can also network within female organizations to compensate for not having the same networking opportunities as their male counterparts. While this approach helps women find others they can relate with, Julie has experienced somewhat diminishing returns as these organizations can become too insular which makes it difficult to build new relationships through them. It also does not solve the problem that men still make most of the decisions in the professional world, so you must network with them as well. In some ways, women's organizations actually exacerbate the problem, because you wind up spending all of your networking time with women who aren't necessarily making all of the impactful decisions. It is important to network with both genders to fully integrate yourself within your professional environment.

* * *

While Julie refuses to golf, Laura Rogers loves the sport.

Many consider golf the ultimate old boy's club. Throughout Laura's time as a golfer, she has consistently been one of the few girls, if not the only one, at every step of the process.

She began golfing as a young child with her dad. Beginning when she was five, he would bring her to the driving range to hit balls. As she grew older, he began taking her to play nine holes, and eventually to play eighteen. Over the years, she participated in golf camps and training sessions and has been on a variety of golf teams.

In middle and high school, she played on the junior league co-ed team for a local golf course. This team mostly consisted of boys. Typically, there were one or two other girls, but the rest of the team was guys. The camps that she attended were also always dominated by boys.

In high school, she also played on her school's varsity girls golf team. While there was both a boys' and a girls' team, the boys team had about 40 kids try out, while the girls' team only had about 17 kids try out. This vast discrepancy shows how few girls play golf.

In college, Laura is the only girl on a team of around twenty-five golfers.

Laura emphasizes how intimidating it can be as the only girl. One of her first goals upon entering college was to try out for the co-ed club golf team. She ended up the only girl on the team. At times, she finds it difficult to fit in. Normally very outgoing, she is much more reserved and quiet in situations when she is the only girl among all of the guys.

While the boys do try to include her, like the boy on her team who specifically chose her as his partner in tournaments, she still often feels isolated. In the past, when there is another girl playing on her team, Laura will typically stick with her, as there is a sense of camaraderie among women in golf. Given that there is no other girl on her current team, it is difficult to form those relationships.

Laura manages to ameliorate this problem by joking with them and talking the way that they talk, but she still feels weird being the only girl.

Her golf talent has also impressed many of the guys, which helps her fit in with them. Most of the time, before they see her play, men assume that she is a bad golfer because she is a woman. They are shocked when they see that she can play quite well, and will make comments about how good she is. Once she shows she can play, it is easier to blend in with the boys and she is able to gain their respect.

Laura also possesses a great deal of knowledge about sports, particularly about golf. This makes it easier to bond with the guys, as sports is a common topic of conversation for them. Her golf knowledge allows her to talk about subjects like who is playing in a tournament on any given weekend, which helps her fit in the male-dominated environment.

Laura also spent time working as cart staff at a golf course with one of her female golfer friends. The cart staff are responsible for carrying people's bags to and from carts. Laura and her friend were the first girls to take on this job at their golf course. Their experience was very different from that of the boys who worked the very same job. The two of them made over $200 in tips in a couple hours on the job, whereas the boys would have made around $10 in tips during this same time frame. Many of the men would not allow the girls to carry their bags and the ones that did would tip them $10, when they would have tipped a boy either nothing or $1. Some of the men that came to golf at the course would make comments to the girls, such as the time when Laura's teenage friend was told by a much older man that his golf bag had never looked as good as it did while she was carrying it. The girls had to deal with many comments about their appearances, but typically they chose to laugh it off instead of saying something or retaliating, because they wanted to ensure that they would receive tips.

On the LPGA tour, women are expected to dress a certain way (i.e. short golf skirts and low-cut tops) in order to gain viewers, particularly male viewers. Obviously, male golfers do not face this expectation.

There are still golf courses that don't even allow women to play. While there are very few of these left, many other courses have only started allowing women in the last few years. The Augusta National Golf Club, which holds the Masters ever year, did not allow women until 2012.

Golf is an activity that actively discriminates against women. This is a major problem for women when it comes to networking because the old boys club associated with golf limits women's abilities to participate. Many business events take place on the golf course, which is exclusionary towards women, particularly when they aren't even allowed on the grounds.

* * *

Women continually need to find ways to break into these traditionally male areas, particularly because their exclusion puts them at an extreme disadvantage. That being said, men need to do a better job of including women in networking and team-bonding activities in order to promote more equality between genders in the workforce.

Encouraging social activities that are more inclusive to everyone is a great way to combat this issue. Going to dinner, seeing a show, or doing an escape room are all fun bonding activities that allow everyone to participate.

If you feel like you are being left out by the men around you, don't be afraid to ask to join them! I do so all the time. If my guy friends are going to the gym to play a game of basketball, I have no problem asking them to let me join. If you genuinely don't want to do what they are doing, don't force yourself to, but if you are at all interested, go for it!

CHAPTER 8

SPEAK THE LANGUAGE

———

"I like to hang with the boys and I like to prove that I can be one of the boys, if not better."

—MICHELLE BORTH, ACTRESS

* * *

Mary Smith was working to package a company and sell it to another company in South Africa. At the time, Mary was the 40th employee in the United States for the company. Over the last 20 years since the sale, the company has grown to over 30,000 employees.

The entire time she worked on this project, Mary was pushing boundaries. The South African company was very paternalistic. She was forced to find ways to become one of the guys. She had the men she worked with call her by her last name, instead of by her first name because it made it easier for them to get along with her and see her as one of them.

It was critical for her to maintain her status as one of the guys because all of the growth in the company happened in sales and engineering. If you weren't in those areas, and instead were in a more traditionally female role such as human resources or marketing, then you would miss out on the action. If you wanted the company to consider you an essential part of their strategy, you had to ensure that you could hang with the men.

* * *

In her article "Speaking While Female," Sheryl Sandberg, along with Adam Grant, highlight what communication in the workplace can look like for women. They share the story of two young women who were working on writing a TV show. In meetings, their producer noticed that they did not speak up, so he encouraged them to do so. Every time they did, a male writer would interrupt.[23]

---

23 Sandberg, Sheryl, and Adam Grant. 2015. "Speaking While Female". *The New York Times*. https://www.nytimes.com/2015/01/11/opinion/sunday/speaking-while-female.html.

This is not an unusual experience for women. Women are interrupted so frequently at work that there is even a term that has been coined to describe it— manterrupting. There are even times when women will have a good idea that is ignored and then a man will say the same thing and it is praised. This is extremely discouraging to women and often lessens their participation in conversations.[24]

I know firsthand how frustrating this is. When I am surrounded by men, I often find it hard to get a word in edgewise. Even when I am able to do so, I am often interrupted or ignored before I am done speaking. Even more frustrating is when I say something and no one responds, but a guy will say the same thing a minute later and everyone agrees with him. One time, I suggested that my guy friends and I all go to a restaurant. Nobody said anything or really cared that I had spoken. One of the guys suggested that we go to the exact same restaurant that I had recommended not even two minutes before and everyone stood up and prepared to leave. These experiences are immensely frustrating for women and men often don't even realize what they are doing.

You might think that the solution to this issue is for women to speak more loudly or aggressively to gain attention. Unfortunately, women have to struggle to find a balance between

---

24 Ibid.

not speaking and seeming too aggressive. A Yale psychologist did a study on the differences in perception of communication of males and females. She found that when professionals were asked to evaluate the competence of their CEOs, male executives that spoke more frequently than their peers were rated to be 10% more competent. Female CEOs that spoke more than their peers received ratings that were 14% lower.[25] This shows that women are penalized for speaking up, which discourages their participation.

This is a problem that needs to be resolved. Women have a lot to offer and are not being given the opportunities to speak up. When they do, they are punished for it and are seen as too aggressive. Having more women in leadership is one major solution to this problem. In the meantime, paying attention to the way men communicate with each other can help women.

I have learned the importance of speaking in a similar way as men. In my friendships with guys, I have adapted to their senses of humor and the unique way that they speak to each other in order to make myself one of them. I have found that one of the ways guys communicate with each other is through gentle teasing. It is not meant in a cruel way, but rather as a way of bonding. For example, when guys are

25 Sandberg, Sheryl, and Adam Grant. 2015. "Speaking While Female". *The New York Times*.

playing each other in beer pong, they tend to poke fun at each other if they throw a poor shot. I learned early on in my friendships with guys that this teasing helps me become one of the guys. It shows the guys that they can do the same thing to me, which makes them more comfortable.

This is a great tactic in the workforce. As women start to get comfortable with their male coworkers, they can have a little fun and interact in the same ways that they see the men doing. Obviously, work banter will be very different from what goes on in casual social settings between friends, but the same idea still applies.

An unfortunate part of banter with men is hearing sexist jokes. While my guy friends are typically very respectful of women, they do have their moments where they make jokes about women and women's abilities. These types of jokes don't bother me because I know that my friends do not at all mean them seriously or believe that women are not capable of greatness. However, while these jokes do not bother me personally, I think they are part of the culture that makes women uncomfortable in male environments, particularly in the workplace. When men say these types of things, even though they may not be ill-intentioned, they can have negative consequences. This type of humor reinforces the idea that women are lesser than men. While most men likely do not consciously believe the content of these jokes, this attitude still contributes to the subconscious biases about women's abilities to perform traditionally male jobs and tasks.

This is something that I struggle with personally. I never know whether I should call out a guy for making a sexist joke or if I should laugh along with it and let it go. Often, I take sort of a middle ground, where I jokingly scowl at the offender. This lets him know that I don't approve of what he is saying, without making a big deal of it or removing my status as one of the boys.

This may not be the best permanent solution, and as I enter the workforce myself, I am going to work towards calling these instances out when I see them, instead of just allowing it to happen and perpetuating a culture in which women are seen as lesser than men.

* * *

Learning to interact with men in the way that they interact with each other has been immensely helpful to me when it comes to fitting in with a group of guys. When you are in a male-dominated environment, pay attention to how the guys communicate with one another. Imitation is your best friend here. I'm not saying you should change who you are or what you want to say, rather change how you go about saying it. Learn the male lingo and try to use it in a way that works naturally for you.

CHAPTER 9

PROMOTE DIVERSITY

"All men benefit from an America where men hold the power and women are largely excluded from it."

—*AMY NELSON, ENTREPRENEUR AND LAWYER*

* * *

Lisa, the executive at IBM from earlier in the book, charged her team with creating a weekly publication for the practitioners in the business unit. In the first issue of the newsletter, there was a link to a video by Lisa, welcoming everyone to the first issue of the newsletter. Shortly after publishing the newsletter, Lisa received an email from one of the practitioners. The practitioner let Lisa know that he was deaf and therefore the video was not very useful to him.

As Lisa tells the story, she had not until then, been acquainted with anyone who was deaf. So despite her focus on and passion for Inclusion & Diversity, she made a mistake in not being expansive enough in her thinking. This error on her part was a learning experience that ended up being an extremely valuable lesson. The individual who informed her of her mistake has helped her and the team promote a broad understanding of the value of inclusion to drive diversity. She points to the quote "Diversity is a fact. Inclusion is a choice" to underscore the value of inclusive thinking.

Ultimately, the deaf man who informed Lisa of her mistake has become one of her advisors. This error on her part was a learning experience that in the end was extremely valuable. He has helped her immensely in her efforts to promote inclusion and diversity at her company and has led her to a broader understanding of those with different needs from her own. Lisa emphasizes the importance of studying our failures. She believes that you can learn a lot from the mistakes that you make.

It is extremely important that we take the time to consider the situations of those around us. Oftentimes, when we do not experience something ourselves, we do not even realize it happens. This occurs over and over again for women in the workplace, as men have vastly different experiences and do not always realize when women are enduring something negative. This same thing happens for other groups of people as well, not just women.

Diversity promotes the ability to recognize our own unconscious biases. We all have unconscious biases as a result of the way we grew up. For example, if you neutralize a series of resumes by removing names and then add the names, they will be ranked differently each time due to the reviewers unconscious bias. We need to understand our own unconscious biases and drive them out of our decision-making processes.

* * *

Sam works as an Associate Producer at a news organization. At her current job, she is primarily surrounded by other women. She is much calmer and more comfortable working with other women, particularly when asking questions. In her experience, asking female colleagues a question is much friendlier interaction and has less of a power dynamic than going to a male colleague. Women that she has worked with have been less patronizing and intimidating than men she has worked with. Her female colleagues, particularly the one who had the job before Sam did, are extremely willing to help her out as much as she needs. This has not always been true of her male coworkers.

In her earlier position as an intern at a different news organization than the one she currently works for, Sam had an experience with a male colleague that made her extremely uncomfortable. She asked a question about the rollout of a show she was working on and he responded in a patronizing and rude manner, indicating that she should already know the information. She said this made her never want to talk to him again.

This is a perfect example of why more diversity in the workplace is essential. Everyone should have coworkers that they feel comfortable going to for help when necessary. With more women in the workplace, women will have more opportunities to interact with people with whom they feel comfortable, rather than feeling intimidated by having to rely on someone they are worried may judge them or brush them off in a condescending manner.

This experience was not the only one where Sam was made to feel uncomfortable by a man in her workplace. On one occasion, she fell through a chair at home and had bruises all over her legs. A male colleague came up to her at work and said "I see you have a bruise on your calf. Is something happening to you outside of work? We have resources to help you if you need anything." Sam responded that she had hurt her leg, but her male colleague kept pressing the issue, saying "no, really if your being hurt by somebody, we can help you."

He was being too insistent and trying to be the savior. She did not feel like it was well-intentioned, and really felt that it was creepy and inappropriate for him to grill her in this manner in the workplace.

This type of behavior is unacceptable. It is one thing to act concerned about a coworker. It is another thing for a man to tell a woman what experiences she is having and what help she needs. It was not this man's place to tell Sam what she needed to do, and it was especially not his place to continue pressing the issue after she told him what had happened.

* * *

Marie Harf also speaks to the importance of diversity. She believes that we need more women in leadership roles, and just more diversity in general in leadership. The more diversity that we have, the fewer of these inclusivity issues we will have.

Marie believes it is promising that a record number of women are running for office this November. A record number of women are donating to campaigns or taking leadership roles in campaigns. This is a positive sign and Marie is hopeful that this pattern will continue and that it will improve the experiences of women in the workplace overall.

She points out that our current leaders need to set a better example. When she thinks about past presidents like George W. Bush and Barack Obama, regardless of their political ideologies, they were both good husbands and fathers to daughters. They both set a good example for the way that people should behave and how they should treat others. She believes that the way that Donald Trump treats women, however, is setting a very bad example for young men in this country. She notes that you see anecdotal stories about teenage boys, and even about younger boys, using his language which is extremely concerning. We need leaders that do better. In the last year alone, a number of powerful men have been fired from their positions due to their treatment of women. Some have been fired too late, but things are changing.

* * *

Lynn Hurley works in the construction industry, which is extremely male-dominated. She experiences how frustrating it is when she needs people to listen to her, and none of the men surrounding her are. Because of this, she occasionally feels under-appreciated. In her experience men do not hand out appreciation or compliments as readily as women do. They also only tend to praise each other, such as when they give each other high fives after accomplishing something. Lynn believes this is either because men do not know how to praise a woman or they are uncomfortable doing so, likely out of fear of being seen as coming on to her. This is a challenge she has faced in a male-dominated field. She has had to grow to accept it because she does not believe it is a reality she can change. It is important to get more women in the field to help combat this problem, as the more women there are, the more praise there will be and the more normal it will become for the men to praise the women as well. She also believes that company training through roleplaying could be a vehicle for teaching men ways to praise women. Lynn feels that the best way to improve this, however, is for some of the guys to step up and just do it to show the other guys that it is okay to congratulate women for a job well done.

She has observed that as the generations change and more women enter the construction field, they are coming in with more education in construction and a better understanding of the job, whereas she learned everything she knows about construction through her work.

The younger men working their way up also seem more sensitive than in the past. They appear more able than older men in the field to have conversations with female coworkers about why women may not feel appreciated and they are more likely to ask what women need to feel comfortable and accepted. As the older men retire, Lynn is seeing this change and is very happy about it, as this is a necessary shift in order to attract more women to the field.

More women taking construction jobs is important. In order to fix the male-dominated culture in the construction industry, they must hire more females in management roles. Lynn still very much sees a glass-ceiling in her industry, even more so than in other industries. The problem lies in the lack of women entering construction. If there are extremely low numbers of women entering the field, then there are not enough to choose from for executive positions, and therefore no one will choose them. In addition, more women entering the field makes it a more accepting place for even more women. The construction industry will improve if more women dive in and take the risk of entering such a male-dominated industry, because this will ease the gender-balance.

Currently construction is very hard on women, particularly at the beginning of their careers. Lynn believes that women are not always given a fair shake. At first, the guys that Lynn was working with did not want to give her the time of day. Lynn is pretty tough, so she did not let this get to her. She spoke with them and told them to give her a chance and some time to prove herself. They complained that she was the third woman who had been hired into the position. The two before her were unsuccessful and had left, so they felt tired of the company bringing in an employee just because she was a woman. Lynn treated this as a fair criticism. There were plenty of qualified men that the company could have hired in place of her, but they wanted a woman in a project management role.

While Lynn was able to gain the respect of her guys and succeed in her role, she has seen many younger women come in who were unable to do so. Her job is to manage projects assigned to her by the management above her. Oftentimes, an inexperienced person will be given smaller, less important jobs. Many women that try to do Lynn's job are held down at these less important jobs for long periods of time and are not challenged or given projects that could improve their experience level. They are held at lower performance levels, whereas the guys tend to receive the opportunity to show off their abilities with larger projects.

* * *

To create a fair and equitable working environment for women, it is most important to improve diversity. The more diverse an organization, the wider the range of perspectives is. This leads to greater understanding of differences and obstacles faced by others and allows people to behave more empathetically towards one another.

Getting more women into fields that are traditionally male-dominated will improve the environment for women in the future and will help create workplaces that are comfortable for everyone.

PART 4

COMMUNITY

CHAPTER 10

FIND MENTORS— MALE OR FEMALE!

———

"When you look at successful women, they have other women who have supported them, and they've gotten to where they are because of those women."

—SHERYL SANDBERG, FACEBOOK COO

* * *

While working at a very male-dominated company in a very male-dominated field, Hannah has been comforted and supported by her extensive network of female mentors. Having women to turn to has made her job much easier and more pleasant. Though her current company is similar to other engineering companies in that it has few female employees, it has an amazing women's network. The company acknowledges that there is a lack of women in the industry and has established a mentor program for female engineers so that their voices can be heard. This provides them with an avenue to learn from one another how to tackle difficult situations in the workplace.

In Hannah's experience, female engineers tend not to vocalize themselves as much as male engineers do. A lot of the program is trying to coach women on behaviors that they have never learned before. Hannah has experienced how men tend to interrupt women. She has learned to be a little more stern at times, even though that is not really in her nature. Along with this she has learned assertiveness and how to set boundaries for herself. She used to feel as though she had to say yes to every request that came her way, however, now she knows this is not the case. She has limited time just like the person next to her, so she can't say yes to every task. This has been a personal internal struggle for her to learn these new behaviors and set those boundaries for herself, especially because this is not a skill society teaches women from a young age.

In college, Hannah found her women's network through Greek life. While at many schools the main purpose of sororities is to party and maintain a social network, Greek life at

MIT is very different. It focuses on making each girl a better person and making MIT a little easier to attend. Hannah was given the opportunity to meet older female mentors that helped her with classes, internships, and jobs. A couple of mentors from her sorority work with her now at her current company. They remain in touch and have helped her manage career moves and work on projects.

Hannah also has mentors she has met through the coveted women's network at her company. She typically grabs lunch with them every week or so to talk about the struggles of work life, where the company is going, and their futures. While they are her professional mentors, Hannah also considers these women to be her friends.

Having strong female mentors has been instrumental in Hannah's success but she also has some wonderful male mentors in her life. One of her long-time mentors was her male high school robotics coach. He has kept up with her since she left high school and they get coffee every time she goes back home for a holiday. Every time she speaks with him she learns so much. She leaves each meeting thinking "Wow, I can do anything."

Hannah's mentors have helped her immensely, which is why she has been willing to help others in the same way. A lot of young women in high school and college have reached out to Hannah for help with resumes, landing an internship, or just with being a female engineer in general. Hannah has really enjoyed giving back to these girls in the same way that her mentors did for her. She is currently mentoring four or five girls on a regular basis. She Skypes each of them every month or so. One girl that she mentors lives all the way in Norway. They were put in contact with one another about three years ago, and Hannah's mentee is about to come visit Hannah and meet her in person.

* * *

Emily, the strength and conditioning coach, could not have gotten to her position today without the help and encouragement of her mentors along the way. Her first mentor was her trainer who began helping her with strength and conditioning when she was 14. At the time, she did not realize the impact that he would have on her and her career. He truly helped mold the person that Emily is today by setting her up for her career, helping her to realize her passion, and encouraging her to take the necessary steps to make her dream a reality.

Another mentor that Emily has found along the way was a college basketball coach that she worked for as a strength trainer. Emily has always known that she comes from a different standpoint than many people. Much like the other women in this book, Emily has always wanted to be the best at every single thing she does in her life. This has driven her to success, even though she works in a heavily male-dominated environment. Emily found that this basketball coach had a similar mentality. It was fun for her to cross paths with someone who shared her outlook. This helped the two to work extremely well together and to enjoy working together.

Finding people who share similar beliefs, ideals, and values is extremely important, especially when you face challenges. Having mentors and friends you can strongly relate to will provide you with advice when you need it the most. Emily found that having these mentors with a shared mentality made her job easier and more enjoyable. It also acted as a crucial element in forming a successful career.

* * *

Weightlifter, Camille Brown, has also found great comfort in her mentors. While she went to the gym only with boys, Camille went to an all-girls high school. She was barely 100 pounds and was constantly trying to gain muscle and gain weight, while everyone else at her all girl's high school was trying to lose weight and become skinnier. They would say if your rib cage showed in your bathing suit, that was attractive. Camille, on the other hand, was working on building muscle in the gym along with the guys.

This created body issues for Camille because people had very different expectations for what an attractive body was at school versus at the gym. It was hard for her to exist in her own world. She felt out of place at school because she would have cuts and bruises from diving in the dirt during softball and she was building muscles throughout her body that none of the other girls had. She felt out of place at the gym as a girl in a group of boys. She worried that she couldn't hang with them. While at school, girls had no trouble speaking up in class for a pad or tampon when they were on their period, in the gym this created insecurity for Camille. She would worry about whether the guys could see the pad she was wearing. She also was uncomfortable telling male coaches that she was experiencing cramps, which led to discomfort while training.

Her goals and her mentors were really what drove her to break through these body image barriers. She was getting faster and stronger. She was able to do pull-ups as a sophomore in high school, which gave her a lot of confidence. This made her not care as much if her quads were bigger than the other girls at her school, or if a guy at the gym told her she ran like a girl.

Her female coach was instrumental in helping Camille get through this time. The coach meshed really well with the men in the gym and found it easy to communicate with the male coaches, who saw her as an equal. She was extremely genuine and was well-respected for her knowledge. It didn't feel like she was a female coach, it just felt like she was a coach because of her skill and qualifications.

Camille was extremely inspired by this coach. As another woman in the weight room, she was someone that Camille could really look up to. This coach could also relate to Camille on a different level than her male coaches and peers. When Camille was insecure about something, such as having calluses, her coach would remind her that it didn't matter and would instruct her to complete more pull-ups. When Camille brought up appearance issues, this female coach always had the perfect, funny thing to say that would make Camille less insecure. She would say things like "wouldn't you rather be able to do ten pull-ups than not have calluses?" She was able to understand the female insecurities that Camille faced in a way that the men in the gym could not.

To help Camille get over her insecurities, her mentor reminded her how much she loved knowing she could show up the asshole in her class. Even better, Camille loved thinking about how all of the coaches would give him shit for losing to her. She also reminded herself of her goals. She thought of how badly she wanted to perform a 200 pound back squat and how she wanted to be faster on the field so that she could make that diving catch in softball.

Camille has begun to help other people break the barrier of worrying about whether their jeans will fit if they squat 200lbs. She preaches that when you focus on your goals, your insecurities will melt away.

When she started really gaining confidence with her performance, she began to face negativity from her softball teammates. She faced negativity from other girls because they thought she was showing off. Camille worked hard for her body and was proud of it. When she would practice in a sports bra, her teammates would make comments to her. She lost friends over social media posts about her progress. Instead of supporting her, many of her female teammates tore her down, which was incredibly difficult to bear. She found herself turning towards the guys she lifted with and her coaches for support instead, as they encouraged her to perform to the best of her abilities.

At the end of the day, who cares what others think of you. People are going to judge you no matter what. Do what you enjoy for yourself, not for anyone else.

Before she started lifting, people judged Camille for being too skinny and too weak and too slow for an athlete. After she decided to do something about it and start lifting, they then started judging her for being too lean, too muscular, and having too much of a six pack. No matter what you do, you are never going to please everyone, you just have to do it for you. Working to meet someone else's expectations doesn't work because then you won't stick with it when you face challenges. The only way to make a long-term commitment is to set goals for yourself that you care about and work toward because of how badly you want them.

* * *

When Madeline, the salesperson at the computer software company from earlier in the book, started on the sales team, she was assigned to one of the other women on the floor who served as Madeline's mentor. This woman was a "badass and didn't take shit from anybody." Madeline learned a lot from her. This woman was on a team of ten guys and they would often try to poke fun at her, but she was fierce and would stand up for herself. She was an awesome role model to Madeline. She had held Madeline's position before Madeline and had not enjoyed her experience so she worked hard to help Madeline through it so that she would succeed and actually enjoy her time working there.

Use your mentor(s) like Madeline did. See what they do to find success and do your best to imitate what behaviors drive their success. Ask your mentor what strategies have worked best for them (and also what doesn't work), so that you can use the tools that they have developed throughout their careers.

* * *

Lisa Mascolo shares the story of Condoleezza Rice as an example of the importance of mentorship—and the value of mentors who are not like you. Condoleezza Rice went to the University of Denver where she initially majored in music. While she has never lost her passion for music and the piano in particular, at University she began to wonder if her talent in this area was enough to make a career. Subsequently she attended an international politics course taught by someone who encouraged her interest in policy and diplomacy. She developed a long and rewarding relationship with this person who mentored her throughout her career. Ms. Rice's mentor was neither female, nor African American. He was Josef Korbel, a white man of Jewish descent, the father of Madeleine Albright.

Lisa's point in retelling this story is to emphasize what Condoleezza Rice tells many—do not forego mentors who do not look like you. Take advantage of the diversity of thought and experience around you.

* * *

Personally, I have been blessed with both male and female mentors in martial arts. My first instructor, who taught me from when I started at the age of five through my teenage years, was extremely critical to my development as a martial artist. Not only was he a great instructor, but also a great mentor and friend. He always encouraged me to fulfill my potential in martial arts, as well as in other aspects of my life. He consistently praised me for my karate and my academic abilities. He also did a wonderful job of putting the guys I was in class with in their place. He always would say that "girls are better at karate than boys." Every time he said this, it motivated me to prove him right. He is someone who kept me going, even when I was challenged by the boys. Knowing that he believed in me pushed me to be my best.

There were also some extremely talented girls older than I was that trained at the karate school. I really looked up to them as I grew up. Seeing how strong and badass they were inspired me to keep training so that one day I could be as good as they were.

Having mentors, whether male or female, is extremely important to the success of women in male-dominated fields. Mentors serve as a guide and a stable rock for women to lean on as they move through their careers.

CHAPTER 11

GIVE BACK

———

"Every one of us has the power and obligation to be a champion for girls around the world."

—MICHELLE OBAMA, FORMER FIRST LADY

* * *

Be willing to turn around and help the next girl.

When Mary Smith was in a marketing position, she ran into a woman that did not want her to be successful. She had a performance review with this manager and the manager told Mary that she was a mediocre performer, even though Mary knew she was the top performer. Mary stopped the review and said "I don't trust you and you don't trust me, so this review is over. I would like your support in finding another job in this company, but if I have to leave the company I will. I want you to know that I am not listening to any more of this." and she stood up and walked out of the room.

It was really eye-opening for Mary to see how she was treated differently not only by men, but also by women. This is particularly apparent in cases where there are women working in more traditionally female roles, such as marketing and human resources. These women can get defensive when they see other women getting ahead.

Mary has found that this animosity starts to hit women at the managerial level, which is usually around when they turn thirty. That is the point where it appears as though there is not enough to go around and women get sharp elbows towards one another. While this is happening, the men in these positions are entirely oblivious because they do not experience the same tension.

While Mary has faced hostility from other women, she also has had strong women supporting her throughout her career. When her job was to run the alliance between her company and a major tech firm, the tech firm had just hired a new CEO. Previously, the leadership team consisted almost entirely of men. These men worked independently and consistently tried to outdo one another. The leadership team was extremely competitive and macho. The new CEO came in and fired the entire leadership team and brought in a new group made up half of women and half of other people from diverse backgrounds. This shifted the entire culture of the tech company's leadership.

Think back to Mary's story about the man who brought her to a strip club and how it found its way back to the women on the leadership team at his company and he was out of his job within six months. Having women involved in leadership is incredibly important. Who knows if a group of male leaders would have reacted in the same way.

Based on this story and her other experiences throughout her career, Mary emphasizes the importance of spotting the senior women in an organization and becoming friends with them because they will look out for you, like many of the senior women she became friends with did for her. She is always willing to help out any junior woman she encounters because she has benefitted from women who did the same for her. Women are not always your friend, but if a woman is in a senior role, chances are she has had to lean on others and will help you.

* * *

Riki Tyminski spent time in the Marine Corps. While she often faced disrespect from male marines, she also faced issues from other female marines. On her first day in her fleet, one of the senior women called her the "new bait" and implied that she would sleep around with the men. She expected to face this type of behavior from the men, but was shocked to face it from a fellow woman, who had likely gone through many of the same experiences that Riki would go through. Given that there are so few women in the marines, Riki had expected that they would stick together. While it is often the case that women support each other, there are cases like this one where women can attempt to tear one another down. Instead of letting this situation cause her to give up, Riki used the negativity as motivation to prove herself and succeed. She used it as a mechanism to better herself, instead of allowing it to consume her.

While Riki did face some issues with female marines, there were also many supportive women in the Marine Corps that helped Riki along the way. Riki even met her best female friend in the Marine Corps. Looking to support other women in male-dominated fields is extremely important. It allows for a sense of camaraderie that makes all involved happier and healthier.

Given the way that she has been treated by some women, Riki is always sure to treat other women with respect and is very willing to lend a hand when necessary. It's incredibly important to support other women, particularly in male-dominated fields, as there typically is not enough support for women in these areas. Always stand up for other women, even if other women have not always been there for you.

* * *

As I rose up in the ranks of martial arts, I became an instructor to younger students. I always focused on encouraging my female students and helping them become awesome martial artists. Knowing the impact that my mentors had on me, I tried to do the same for my students, particularly the girls. I always encouraged the girls when they went up against the boys and always let them know that they were just as good, if not better than the guys.

Giving back is a crucial responsibility. We need more women to enter male-dominated fields, particularly in leadership positions in order to improve the workforce for everyone. Women need to help guide other women and serve as a support system, rather than tearing each other down.

CONCLUSION

—

"Women belong in all places where decisions are being made...
It shouldn't be that women are the exception."

—RUTH BADER GINSBURG, SUPREME COURT JUSTICE

* * *

Despite the difficulty, the situation is improving for women in male-dominated fields. As more women enter these fields, more women will work their way up to leadership roles, which will improve the situation even more.

For all of the shit that millennials get, they generally seem to be a more open-minded generation than those in the past. They have grown up in a time where gender equality is important and becoming the expected standard.

According to a study by the Intelligence Group, over two-thirds of people ages 14 to 34 say gender no longer defines destiny or behavior as it once did.[26] This indicates that a majority of millennials believe the gender disparity is improving.

Women are increasingly perceived as capable of traditionally male jobs. In recent years, for example, we have seen women allowed to work in combat roles in the army. We have also seen more women elected to public office.

While men still hold a majority of leadership roles, a study by the Harvard Business Review shows that women are actually rated as more effective leaders by bosses, peers, and subordinates than men. At every level of position surveyed, women were ranked as performing better overall as leaders than their male counterparts. Women were also ranked higher in all but one of the sixteen top competencies displayed by top leaders.[27]

---

26 "Millennials And Gender: A Major Attitude Shift". 2018. *The Atlantic*. https://www.theatlantic.com/sponsored/prudential-sleeping-giants/millennials-and-gender-a-major-attitude-shift/467/.

27 Zenger, Jack, and Joseph Folkman. 2012. "Are Women Better Leaders Than Men?". *Harvard Business Review*. https://hbr.org/2012/03/a-study-in-leadership-women-do.

This shows that women are good at what they do— often better than men. We should broadly distribute this information to help increase the number of women in leadership positions. We should encourage more women to go into STEM fields, business, government, and other male-dominated fields because women have a lot to offer and can revolutionize these industries.

When asked what it is like to coach a girl, Becca Longo's college football coach says "I don't coach girls, I coach football players."[28] This outlook shows that he sees Becca in the same light as his male players and that he holds her to the same standards as the boys. Men should take note from leaders like this coach. Women alone cannot fix perception problems. Men are the ones that hold much of the power, therefore they must participate in this gender revolution for it to succeed.

To Men: Listen to the women in your lives. Listen to the obstacles that they face and the harassment that they deal with. Ask questions when you don't understand what they are going through. Try to put yourself in their shoes. Encourage them to be their best. Never assume that they can't or won't want to do something because of their gender. Recognize implicit biases that you may possess. Take them into consideration when making hiring or promotion decisions. If you

---

28 "Female Football Powerhouse". 2018. *Facebook.*

have children, remember that they are just as much yours as they are hers. Even if you don't have children, realize the discrimination in the workforce that exists for women who do. Finally, don't be afraid to call out other men for sexist behavior or remarks. Women do not always feel comfortable standing up for themselves. You may not enjoy it either, but it is a lot easier for you to tell a male coworker to knock it off than it is for a woman.

To Women: You are strong and capable of accomplishing anything that you set your mind to. Find what you are passionate about and pursue it with all of your heart. Never give up and never back down. You are deserving of success. Don't be afraid to be the only girl in the room. Use others' doubts about you to motivate you to be your best self. Surround yourself with people who support you and your goals. Encourage other women. Always be willing to help the next girl behind you.

The bottom line is that as we have more women in leadership, we will have more equality and the situation will continue to improve. Women are extremely capable, sometimes more-so than men, and offer not only many of the same skills but also some unique talents and perspectives. Never underestimate a woman in any field.

ACKNOWLEDGEMENTS

———

I never thought that I would write anything nearly as long as a book, never mind become a published author. I have had so much support throughout this process and could never have accomplished this without all of the amazing people in my life.

Thank you to my parents for supporting me in everything I do! You have always pushed me to be the best person I can be and you have taught me to persevere through any challenges that I have come across. A huge shoutout to my sister, Laura, for always being there for me and for always ensuring that I am fed by bringing me food when I don't have the time.

Thank you to Max who was my rock and biggest supporter throughout this entire process. You were always there whenever things got difficult or I had doubts about my ability to finish this thing. You read and (very thoroughly) edited my book from cover to cover, even though you had a million other things to be doing. I love and appreciate you more than you could ever know.

I would like to thank all of my friends who have endured me talking about this book nonstop over the past year. Special thanks to my roommates, Morgan, for being so supportive and for reading and editing the final version and Lindsay, for always checking in on me and asking about my progress on this project. I love you guys so much and could not have done it without either of you!

To every single woman I interviewed throughout this process, thank you for all being so kind and willing to help me, even though I was a random stranger from the internet. While I couldn't include all of your stories, each and every single one of you inspired me and contributed to the book. Chris, Julie, Kelly, Camille, Lisa, Hannah, Rachel, Marina, Madeline, Marie, Lynn, Sam, Riki, Katie, Federica, Jessica, Kate, Alison, Christal, and Allison, I truly appreciate the time each of you took speaking with me about your experiences.

Finally, I would like to thank Eric Koester, Brian Bies, my editors, my cover designer, and New Degree Press for making the publication of this book a reality.

APPENDIX

INTRODUCTION

Creighton, Jolene. 2018. "Margaret Hamilton: The Untold Story Of The Woman Who Took Us To The Moon". *Futurism*. https://futurism.com/margaret-hamilton-the-untold-story-of-the-woman-who-took-us-to-the-moon.

Miller, Claire, Kevin Quealy, and Margot Sanger-Katz. 2018. "The Top Jobs Where Women Are Outnumbered By Men Named John". *The New York Times* https://www.nytimes.com/interactive/2018/04/24/upshot/women-and-men-named-john.html.

CHAPTER 1

"Can A Woman Play In The NFL?". 2018. *Sports Feel Good Stories.* https://www.sportsfeelgoodstories.com/can-a-woman-play-in-the-nfl/.

"Female Kicker Makes College Football History". 2018. *CNN.* https://www.cnn.com/videos/sports/2017/04/15/female-college-football-kicker-becca-longo-intv-nr.cnn.

Hayes, Martha. 2017. "Hillary Clinton Quotes: The Would-Be President In Her Own Words". *Marie Claire.* https://www.marieclaire.co.uk/entertainment/people/hillary-clinton-quotes-to-make-you-feel-truly-empowered-42730.

"Tackle Your Dreams: 3 Tips From Footballer Becca Longo". 2018. *Youtube.* https://www.youtube.com/watch?v=1yrxSzA6OLo.

CHAPTER 2

Nelson, Amy. 2018. "Moms Are Punished In The Workplace, Even When We Own The Business". *The Washington Post.* https://www.washingtonpost.com/news/posteverything/wp/2018/01/29/i-started-my-own-business-i-still-couldnt-escape-stereotypes-about-working-moms/?utm_term=.207bedbe2ba8.

CHAPTER 6

Cueto, Emma. 2014. "What J.K. Rowling Using A Male Pseudonym Says About Sexism In Publishing". *Bustle.* https://www.bustle.com/articles/15839-what-jk-rowling-using-a-male-pseudonym-says-about-sexism-in-publishing.

Gillett, Rachel. 2018. "From Welfare To One Of The World's Wealthiest Women—The Incredible Rags-To-Riches Story Of J.K. Rowling". *Business Insider.* https://www.businessinsider.com/the-rags-to-riches-story-of-jk-rowling-2015-5.

Greig, Geordie. 2006. "'There Would Be So Much To Tell Her...'". *The Telegraph.* https://www.telegraph.co.uk/news/uknews/1507438/There-would-be-so-much-to-tell-her....html.

Lawless, John. 2005. "Revealed: The Eight-Year-Old Girl Who Saved Harry Potter". *The New Zealand Herald.* https://www.nzherald.co.nz/lifestyle/news/article.cfm?c_id=6&objectid=10333960.

CHAPTER 8

Sandberg, Sheryl, and Adam Grant. 2015. "Speaking While Female". *The New York Times.* https://www.nytimes.com/2015/01/11/opinion/sunday/speaking-while-female.html.

CONCLUSION

"Female Football Powerhouse". 2018. *Facebook*. https://www.facebook.com/Upworthy/videos/10155451851523059/UzpfSTEw-MDAxMDU1NTE4NTU0ODo3NjcoMjkxNTM2MTg5MTc/.

"Millennials And Gender: A Major Attitude Shift". 2018. *The Atlantic*. https://www.theatlantic.com/sponsored/prudential-sleeping-giants/millennials-and-gender-a-major-attitude-shift/467/.

Zenger, Jack, and Joseph Folkman. 2012. "Are Women Better Leaders Than Men?". *Harvard Business Review*. https://hbr.org/2012/03/a-study-in-leadership-women-do.

CPSIA information can be obtained
at www.ICGtesting.com
Printed in the USA
BVHW091443271118
534126BV00011B/115/P